Harry Kernoff

About the Author

Kevin O'Connor is a former radio producer with RTÉ and BBC. He has made hundreds of radio features/documentaries and is the author of other books, including *The Irish in Britain, Ironing the Land: How the Railways Came to Ireland* and *Blake and Bourke*.

Harry Kernoff

The Little Genius

Kevin O'Connor

The Liffey Press

Published by
The Liffey Press Ltd
Raheny Shopping Centre, Second Floor
Raheny, Dublin 5, Ireland
www.theliffeypress.com

A catalogue record of this book is
available from the British Library.

ISBN 978-1-908308-22-1

Printed in Spain by GraphyCems.

Contents

Preface

As Harry Kernoff assumes the spaces reserved for him in private and public places, I reflect that years ago I purchased his whimsical portrait of James Joyce in a basement auction at Adams. That it was consigned to end-of-season told me little then about its subject or creator – I acted on instinct and years passed before I fully realised the worth of both.

Another stretch of years and the art collector Garrett O'Connor suggested a biography. I came to rue that undertaking when meeting obstacles of time and access, but was rewarded on the far side of endurance by encountering so much of Kernoff's art and much that intrigued about his life, always a lure. Help came from niece Kate Kernoff in London and great-nephew Leslie Kernoff in South Africa.

Their generosity in donating family archive to the country he adopted – and which adopted him – was crucial to this work, as is their continuing goodwill, which does not mean they agree with all of my interpretation, a risk endemic in biography. Kernoff was no different from many in keeping bits of his life in separate compartments and nobody knew everything about him. I hope here to have garnished as full a 'picture' as the times allow, though aware there are areas still be explored, just as he did in his art.

Many helped in pursuit of this biography, too numerous or too private to mention. Not all that was given was used and my apologies to those whose pictures or information did not make the final print. Harsh decisions are made to give a representative range of an artist's life and work. Also, dates and methods as to oil, watercolour or pastel have not always been used for the sensible reason that our artist did more than one version of some works and in different media when the market or his own feelings suggested repetition.

Specific thanks are due to Amelia Stein, Ciaran MacGonigal and Robert Ballagh for insights into the cultural context in which Kernoff lived and worked, to Liam Cahill and Ted Walsh, to collectors Liam Slattery, Nigel Bennett, John and Mercy Staunton, Stephanie Walsh, auctioneer Ian Whyte, gallery owners Thérése and James Gorry, artists Bernadette Madden, Tom Ryan, Catriona Ni Threasaigh, and the library staffs of NGI, NPG and NLI. Crucially helpful were Pat Murphy and Dono Romano and their colleagues in National Irish Visual Arts Library at NCAD.

Joan Bergin is thanked for her patience in losing a room in our house to an archive of boxes and catalogues. Emma Burke-Kennedy expertly photographed works from private collections, their owners repaid by The Liffey Press with a generous amount of colour plates – well above the average for our economic times – and of such impact here as to encourage enthusiasts to look further in galleries and auctions, bookshops and bequests, where Kernoff continues to surprise with the panoramic range of his talent.

Kevin O'Connor
Dublin, November 2012

1

The Kernoff Family Arrive in Ireland

A painter's life may tell us little about his art – but his art will certainly tell us about the life. As writers of fiction reveal their inner narrative through their public characters, so the painter's treatment of external subjects unwittingly unleash private concerns.

The inheritance which Harry Kernoff carried in his genes was expressed in his art through bold brushwork, vivid colours and affection for his subjects. As Dublin replaced the Russian town of Vitebsk, from which his parents had fled during the 1890s, the Irish city became his adopted homeplace, the beneficiary of his talent and, in the wider sense, his universe. He lived among and studied its people, recording them in their infinite variety and was rivalled only by James Joyce in bequeathing a narrative of the city. As Joyce departed shortly after the turn of the century, Kernoff was left with a clear palette to record Dublin's complexion as it changed with the century.

By birth a Londoner, by family Russian, by religion Jewish, his paintings show iconic respect for those who impacted upon history in revolutionary times, leavened with warmer affection for the ordinary people who suffer the history.

With playful humour, Kernoff imbues the busy journeymen and women of the Irish streets with a dignity that acknowledges their human endeavour. They hurry to fulfil minor, but to them important, tasks in 'life's rich tapestry' during the twentieth century. His own life and worked spanned exactly three-quarters of that century.

By contrast, when Kernoff turns his hand to commissioned totems or to political portraiture, his subjects are sometimes stilted. One senses anti-establishment resentments skewing his fluidity of line. All, however, had a place in his own life, whether as fee-paying subjects or, as was more often the case, stimulating his personal panorama. Humanity breathes in his work, as did fellow-feeling ordain his own life.

Much of that humanity must have come from his parents, married on the first day of the New Year of 1899, which was also the last year of the nineteenth century. The wedding ceremony at the East London Synagogue was in the heart of a community that settled straight from the ships that brought them from European persecution to the dockside of a liberal and industrial England that needed workers. Katya Burbanel married Isaac Karnov, who was one of three brothers who fled Russia ahead of the Czar's army dragooning for compulsory military service. Both families were also refugees from anti-Semitism in Russia, which, among other manifestations, robbed personal property, ghettoised families and imposed harsh military service upon young Jewish men.

As part of their great migration from mainland Europe, England was meant to be a temporary stop en route to South Africa, where Isaac had relatives, but his marriage to Katya halted his plans. Both partners were strongly Jewish, of the Hasidic tribe, and Katya, being the daughter of a Rabbi, held a certain vanity and awareness of her place in the community. Her family traced its lineage via Russia to the Spanish court of Ferdinand and Isabella, a royal duo whose marital alliance and anti-Muslim and anti-Jewish policies determined European concerns from the middle ages.

According to family pedigree, Katya's ancestor was Chancellor in the court of Ferdinand and Isabella. Don Isaac A'brabanel was a financier who raised funding for Columbus's voyage to North America and for Spanish colonial acquisitions in the South Americas. The expansion of Spanish Catholic power by military might was funded by Chancellor A'brabanel's taxes in Spain and later in the acquired colonies of Central and South America – an imperial exploitation of natives that today resonates in the South Americas under the term of *conquistador*.

Also, according to family legend, which tends to sanitise, Don Isaac 'converted' from Moor to Christian and was later expelled from the Court when opposing the methods used in the conquest of South America, nowadays defined as genocide. Other evidence suggests that his role as State tax-gatherer left him vulnerable to intrigue by syndicates of Spanish merchants who resented a government official of Moorish origin extracting taxes from Christians.

Whatever the truth of the political heave from this distance, the A'brabanel family lore handed down that the Chancellor had departed Spain in fear of his life. His descendants settled in Russia, from whence his family line continued in the town of Vitebsk, which during the 1890s endured a pogrom as the homes and shops of the Jewish population were burned. The parents of Harry Kernoff saw terrifying attacks which prompted their eventual departure from Russia and migration to England.

The painter Marc Chagall, also in Vitebsk, witnessed this pogrom from the attic of his wooden house – harbinger of his later work, done from the safety of Paris, with distortion of human figures airborne above village streets.

Curiously, Kernoff's peopled laneways of Dublin, painted about thirty years later, bear some causal connection to Chagall, illustrating how great artists unleash their unconscious concerns into their work.

Much of this persecuted inheritance was endemic to Katya Abrabanel, the artist's mother, conscious of her descent from Don Isaac, defined in family remembrance as 'Illustrious Safardi', while the men's flight from military service left an abiding anti-imperial impulse in the family culture which would find graphic expression in her son's work. These were some of the inheritances solemnised on the day the painter's parents were married in the United Synagogue of London in 1899, in a ceremony which set out rigourously the duties and rights of both husband and wife. The surviving certificate shows a marriage contract in Hebrew, with English translation on the reverse side. The first child of their union, born a year later, was called Aaron. Two boys and a girl would follow. As often was the case, Aaron (Harry) as the eldest secured a primal place in his mother's heart. It would stand to him.

Harry was an obedient son at home and an effective learner at school. At the age of eleven he was awarded the King's Medal, a weighty lobe of pewter dispersed by London Education Council, for Punctuality and Attendance. Crucial to his later vocation, he displayed an early interest in art, assigned to produce sketches for school sports days and concerts.

The home atmosphere was warm and orderly with an emphasis on knowledge and study. Isaac Karnov was a cabinet maker in the enduring custom of continental Jews who made furniture, a tradition originating in Venice during the Middle Ages when, due to confinement to the ghetto, Jews were barred from banking and turned to furniture-making for the merchant princes. In Dublin, Isaac Karnov would enjoy a reputation for beautiful Venetian chairs.

The Karnov family move in 1914 from London to the Irish capital, then uneasily within the British Empire, was a migration hastened by their menfolk's impending service as conscripts in the Great War, which the family feared would become a repetition of their flight from Russia. Though conscription was imminent in Britain it was being politically resisted in Ireland. While the war would re-make the nation states of Europe at the cost of millions of lives, there was no gain for the Jews. Anti-Semitism was rife within both the French and German empires, now in bitter conflict with each other. Dublin seemed a safer place – according to the letters of relatives, the Irish capital was a city where Jews prospered.

Harry was fourteen in 1914, an adolescent in tandem with the age of the new twentieth century. In that watershed year for Europe he was uprooted across the Irish Sea to a new and strange city – but not to a completely strange environment. The family settled in a Jewish district of Dublin already colonised by migrants and known as 'Little Jerusalem'. In a few square miles of Ireland's capital, Jews from Russia, Latvia and Lithuania had established themselves in the environs of Camden Street, Clanbrasil Street and South Circular Road.

Within weeks of their arrival, Kate Burbanel, as her name had become, cut an imposing figure. A striking-looking woman fashionably turned out and with a flair for turning heads, she would make an impact that would stand to the family's fortunes. Shortly after arrival, she was described as having 'the air of a Spanish Grandee'.

The Karnov family settled at No. 12, Raymond Street, one floor over basement in a terrace of red-brick houses. Within the area were Philly Rubenstein the kosher butcher, Goldberg the baker and Aronvitch the grocer. Clanbrasil Street, a traffic artery spanning the city from North to South, showed Jewish names along its shop fronts. Some of the owners – representing previ-

12 Raymond Street, Dublin 8 – the first Kernoff family home

ous migrations – now lived in substantial homes further south in Terenure under the lea of the mountains. For those with a mind for such designs, the Star of David was common in the fanlights of stained glass over hall doors along streets as Clanbrasil, Portobello and Dolphin's Barn were colonised by migrants. Altogether, the Karnovs arrived into a city supplying the staples of prosperity to their race.

South Dublin's Jewery had schools, two synagogues, various social clubs and charities, sinews of support in a community of several thousand. It was into this network that the Karnov family settled, adapting their name from the Russian Karnov – where the 'v' is pronounced as 'f' – to Kernoff which gave the correct Russian sound in an English-speaking culture. To those of the host community who came to know them, Katya became Kate.

The family consisted of Aaron, the eldest, followed by brothers Herman and Bernard and Lina their sister. Aaron was 'Harry', Herman would be known as Heimie or 'Kay' while Bernard was known as 'Barney'.

As a child in London Harry had shown sustained attachment to his father's work, becoming skilled in wood detail. Unlike today, furniture then was intended for longevity. Fascia had scrolls and filigree, drawers were doweled, panels were bevelled. Motifs requiring artistic skill were inlaid on many woods; mahogany and oak for sideboards and tables. Sustained sellers were bow-fronted cabinets to display wedding presents, then a seminal showpiece in setting-up a middle-class home.

Isaac Karnov expected his furniture to hold heirloom value for future generations. He sold Venetian chairs to the more expensive Dublin shops. Their local synagogue commissioned an Ark, a signal recognition of Isaac's talents and respected place in the community.

It was also expected that the eldest son would be apprenticed to the father and eventually inherit the business, and in that tradition from their move to Dublin in 1914 Harry developed a finesse of hand and eye that unwittingly gave him a head start in draughtmanship.

In Dublin, too, family legend has it that he drew the outline of his father on glass by dipping his finger in butter to use as paint. In fact, he could not be restrained from drawing anybody – and anything – that took his fancy. The walls of the Dublin workshop became filled with his doodles and sketches, annoying Isaac as every surface became a temptation to doodle by his eldest son. Or so the family legend goes...

However, the father's annoyance was tempered by Kate's delight in her first-born's caricatures of the family and proudly showing them to visitors. In his new Irish home, the young Harry Kernoff found, wrapped in a mother's protective love, the first uncritical audience of his artistic vocation. She was already conditioned to his interest, having taken him from Shoreditch to London galleries before his teens, and later to the great repository of Renaissance Art available in the collections of central London.

In Dublin, he announced he would become an artist. Kate approved but Isaac was not as sympathetic, being a taciturn man, a dutiful husband and the sole bread-winner. As was the norm, he left to his wife the running of the household, the conduct of the family budget and decisions of schooling and careers for the children. Whatever his hopes that his eldest son would follow him into cabinet making, he bowed to Kate's insistence that Harry should realise his talent and attend art school. Whatever his feelings of being deprived of an apprentice – and potential inheritor of the business – Isaac's resistance was overruled by his formidable wife.

He did, however, make the case that the boy could not become a day pupil among a wealthy class of students whose fees were paid from merchant coffers. After enquiries were made of the Metropolitan School of Art, it became clear that full-time day attendance did not gel with limited family finances and, as matters came to a head, a compromise determined Harry would continue his apprenticeship to his father and study art in the evening. The decision meant long hours in the father's workshop and another stint in the evening at art lessons. With all that, the family had not quite escaped the volatility of the times.

The period of the family's settling in Ireland, 1914–18, was politically volatile as the Great War drew off hundreds of thousands of young Irishmen into the regiments of the Imperial Army. As two large garrison barracks at Rathmines and Portobello were close to their home, it was usual for the Kernoff boys to see marching ranks of soldiers en route to the Great War cheered on by their families from the slums of Rialto. The boys were also aware that enlisting was opposed by Irish nationalists, resentful of thousands of young men taking the 'King's Shilling' as a release from slums to uniform.

These Irish conflicts had shades of the racial strife that expelled them from Russia. Street meetings opposed conscription for the war as Ireland was divided between factions which saw Imperial Britain taking young men off to kill – and be killed. On this island within the Empire the Ulster, Munster, Connaught and Leinster regiments swelled with adolescents; in Dublin, from warrens of slums near the Jewish area, whole streets of young men enlisted to get a wage and a soldier's regalia. 'Guns and drums' was adventure for young men for whom a shilling marked the end of poverty as they knew it.

These events engaged Harry's interest because of his father and uncles fleeing military conscription in both Russia and England. The seam of socialist fervour which ran in his family would find expression in artistic work as within the Kernoff household was a community sense which found resonance outside.

During 1913, a year before their arrival, there has been a mass agitation by the unemployed, in which the police had battoned marchers. As in many British cities, Dublin was a Victorian contrast of substantial merchants in near proximity to miles of slums with no running water or sanitation. In 1916 those contrasts were to ignite twin seams of agitation – Nationalism and Socialism – which led to a take-over of key installations by armed revolutionaries. In Russia a year later, 1917, a similar armed revolt on a far greater scale would determine European history for the rest of the century.

Fearful of political upheaval spilling into family harmony but determined to make a life for themselves in the midst of chaos, the Kernoff parents stayed close within the Jewish community of the South Circular Road and concentrated on the welfare of their sons and daughter. Four years after his family arrived in Ireland in the autumn of 1918, the family debate over his future having been resolved, Harry Kernoff and his brother Kay enrolled in evening classes at the Metropolitan School of Art.

2

The Metropolitan – 'A Drawing School in Dublin'

The Metropolitan School of Art occupied premises in Kildare Street in the centre of Dublin in high, lofty premises that echoed with history and spilled light on artistic endeavours.

When the Kernoff adolescents, Harry aged 18 and Kay 17 years old, enrolled in the autumn of 1918, evening attendance meant a meal at home and then a walk of thirty minutes or so by the public park of Stephen's Green to the classrooms. They entered an institution which basked in an excellence evolved over two centuries from the 'rationalism' and 'enlightenment' of the 1700s. The arts in general and painting in particular had been much practised and argued over within the school, whose artistic work mirrored life and politics in Ireland.

Boasting a lineage as a drawing school that went back to 1740, making it among the oldest of such schools in Europe, it had a reputation for teaching by classical rote, using Roman and Greek statuary as models for figurative drawing, abiding by Renaissance principles of portraiture and landscape, and emphasising that practical work made for craftsmanship. Among its luminous

The designing room in the Metropolitan School of Art, early 1900s

alumni were painters Walter Osborne and William Orpen, then of international reputation, and to enhance continuity the school offered teaching posts upon graduation to achieving pupils. By the time of Harry and his brother's enrolment, the instruction was carried out by three such teachers – Sean Keating, James Sleator and Patrick Tuohy. Interestingly, among the many former pupils was W.B. Yeats, who became impatient with repetitive drawing of statues and did not wait the mandatory two years before he could engage with human models. Yeats's talents lay elsewhere.

Thousands of competent painters, designers and sculptors received their training at the Metropolitan, which leaned towards competency in technical drawing in order to qualify teachers for regional schools. It had, as a reflection of the times, more female than male pupils, the women being of wealthy families for whom the 'decorative arts' were part of marriage training.

On the painting side, the standard, and aspiration of pupils, derived from the Renaissance and Old Masters – of which Dublin commercial galleries had a notable number – which students were required to study and copy. Such standards were handed on from teacher to pupil, with the better pupils becoming teachers in turn.

By the time Harry enrolled, the Metropolitan, as part of the wider Anglo-Ireland world, was undergoing traumatic change. The First World War had ended with a catalogue of horrors as the country received back its dead and wounded from the Imperial Army while coping with its own continuing guerrilla warfare between the IRA and garrisons of those same British forces.

In general, these were difficult times for the Anglo-Irish, blamed for the Famine of the previous century and confronted with a burgeoning nationalism in the new one; ingredients for academic volatility during Harry Kernoff's years at art school.

Not immune from these upheavals, the school nevertheless maintained impressive achievements with students regularly among the prize-winners of competitions regulated from South Kensington in London, then arbiter of standards in art teaching.

Political upheaval would influence Harry Kernoff's art, though initially he was a model student, eager to learn. Insofar as tradition provides momentum for talent, the 18-year-old Harry Kernoff joined a company of considerable ability. Fellow students included Charles Lamb from Portadown and Maurice MacGonigal from Dublin. The youngest student at 14 years was George Collie, while among the oldest was James Sleator at 32 – all destined to make their mark alongside student painters Norah McGuinness, all of 17-years-old, and Mainie Jellett, admitted the following year at age 22.

What did Harry learn in his initial months? The answer is the pursuit of excellence. As an underpinning or foundation he drew objects and figures from memory and replicated the anatomical sweep of da Vinci and Michelangelo, whose large sculptures were copied by students under the eyes of tutor-artists John Keating, Harry Clarke and Margaret Clarke as well as 'teachers-in-training' Leo Whelan and Tuohy. That convergence of talent made the place hum with ideas and learning.

Harry Clarke, for instance, had 'the students under his spell' according to Nano Reid, who saw 'the ideas flow from his pencil like magic', while other accounts recall Keating stalking his classroom like 'The Master' of old, stern but engaged. The young Kernoff felt Keating could 'see through' his students, gave off an air of calm control and would sometimes complete a student's work with a flourish of his own and a few words of encouragement. A gaunt intense figure of revolutionary intent in politics and art, Keating became a seminal influence on Kernoff, while Tuohy's depressive temperament he found alarming. In their dual role as teachers and as working artists who pursued a vision of becoming great portrait painters, a creative alchemy rubbed off on their students.

All in all, the Metropolitan hummed with industry from ten to three during the day and from seven to nine in the evening, when the Kernoff boys attended. Much of its success was due to George Atkinson, who became Headmaster in Kernoff's first term and from whose strategy he benefited.

A benign educationalist who believed that 'talent will out – but we have to provide the facilities' and a successful painter and etcher in his own right, Atkinson understood the artistic temperament and the 'touches to the tiller' needed in an academy. He would devote much of his adult life to the Metropolitan, not only as a educationalist but in managing the school's survival from its lofty status within Imperial education to becoming a neglected institution of the emerging Irish Free State.

Harry Kernoff thrived in this house of talent, expanding his skills under the tuition of Keating for pure painting, Clarke for decorative design and Atkinson who gave Life classes. There were long sessions of exploration, using pencil, charcoal, crayon and chalk as they sought the approval of Keating, Tuohy and later Oliver Sheppard, a gifted sculptor who was impressed as Kernoff

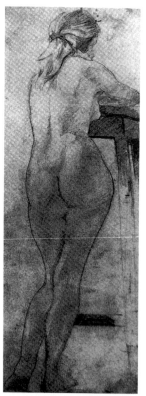

delivered heads and shapes in clay and bronze, though drawing and painting were his primary interests.

It is reasonable to assume that Harry's innate talent was released in the school as skills from childhood doodler to apprentice cabinet-maker had equipped him to be a natural draughtsman. As figurative drawing was rated highly in the classically-biased tradition, his ability to compress fluently between hand and eye impressed Keating, who had inherited such values from Orpen, whom he regarded as 'a world master of draughtsmanship'. Keating in turn passed on the mantle to Kernoff, whose early drawings he called 'the work of a little genius' – a reference to Kernoff's short stature, as Harry was under five and half feet tall.

In painting, Harry learned 'to catch the inner mood' of a subject, as urged by Sleator who by Kernoff's second year had become a junior teacher.

Because the times were politically volatile, academic excellence meshed with profound change. Among his influential teachers, Keating was eleven years older than Kernoff, Tuohy a mere six and Mac-Gonigal was the same age, so that in years and talent they were contemporaries, but it was also clear that Harry absorbed from these fellow artists not only artistic technique but a radicalism to which his Jewish-Russian culture was sympathetic.

Try as it might to keep itself focussed on teaching, the Metropolitan could not function as a rarefied academy, isolated from the volatile times. The ground-swell of Independence from Britain infected all areas of life, as did the aftermath of the Great War and the economic upheavals wrought by thousands of unem-ployable soldiers, the return of the 'trusting and the maimed'. In the few years since Dublin had been devastated by the armed Rebellion against British Rule and emotion-

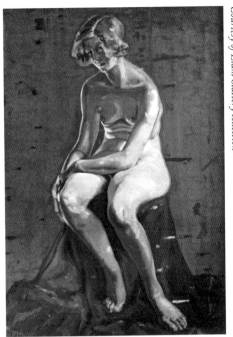

From statuary to real life (previous page) to real women – a nude (above) by Kernoff

ally scarred by the execution of the leaders, tutors Keating and MacGonigal became propagandists for impending Irish nation-hood.

Periodicals and discussion groups harked back to a mythical Ireland of noble warriors (the Fianna) as an emotional platform upon which to build a sovereignty that would bring moral and material well-being, once the imperial shackles to England had been severed. At least that was the theory which infected artists across many disciplines – crafts, painting, sculpture, theatre – in the Celtic Revival intended as a counterculture to Imperial values.

Personal feelings were subject to political pressures. Artists had to choose between Nationalism and Imperialism, or be mar-ginalised from the quickening pulse of the times. It was prophetic to the later course of his artistic work that Harry Kernoff, displaced Jew in Ireland, embarked on adulthood at the same time his adopted homeland floundered towards similar maturity.

Among visitors to the school were Horace Plunkett, pioneer of the co-operative movement which radicalised rural life, and Arthur Griffith, visionary of a 'new' Ireland but virulently anti-Semitic. Among the women students were gun-carrying Republicans of privileged background who managed to combine art studies with also being Suffragettes – with such militancy as to be called 'The Furies'. They frightened most men.

Change was rife in a hotbed of revolution. Ten years before Kernoff set foot in Dublin, James Joyce lolled on the steps of the adjacent library, discussing weighty philosophy and pondering his miserable existence as a prelude to revolutionising the art of fiction. Joyce's earlier short stories were published in Plunkett's magazine, the *Irish Homestead*, while his attendance at classes given by Patrick Pearse were aborted by arguments over language. The ancestors of the Pearse brothers had been stonemasons and political activists in England during the revolution led by Oliver Cromwell, 'first Republican to behead a King'.

The poet W.B. Yeats, not yet a Nobel Laureate, flounced in and out of the art school, whose lofty studios had been frequented by his father John and brother Jack – each a significant painter. Samuel Beckett, Oliver Gogarty, George Moore and George Russell knew the classrooms of the Metropolitan School of Art, as did political leaders Michael Collins and Eamon de Valera who were visitors to students' exhibitions.

If ghosts meant anything to the living, Harry Kernoff's art was brushed by layers of time present with time past. Revolutionary zeal was in the air in Ireland as it had been in the Russia of his parents. In spite of his own sanguine nature, his work could not escape the dramatic forces of Dublin life during the 1920s.

New ways of creativity were being forged in the arts as in politics. Painters as dominant during his student years as Jack Yeats and Paul Henry, influenced by European trends, returned to Dublin with theories on painting as radical as the emerging politics and both became icons for Kernoff's generation of students. Jack Yeats was affected by Picasso and the Impressionists to move away from the classical tradition with its emphasis on natural perspective and lifelike figures.

In Paris, Paul Henry had been strongly affected by the 'fluid collages of intense colour' which he had seen used by Van Gogh. Within the Metropolitan, these trends provoked experimentation. Students and teachers differed, forming cabals of both artistic and political conviction. George Moore and George Russell (AE) joined in the debate on artistic theory, while in the streets outside civic order was also in a state of flux.

As noted, the Ireland that Kernoff encountered in a state of 'chassis', to use O'Casey's phrase, with a questioning what it meant to be British (citizen of Empire, loyal to the Crown) or Nationalist (Independence from Empire, elected Head of State). To oversimplify somewhat, those of a moneyed Protestant background tended to be Imperialists, and regarded the Rebellion of 1916 as a 'stab in the back' to Britain's immense war casualties, whereas Nationalists regarded 'England's difficulty as Ireland's opportunity'.

Exceptions added to the confusion. Thousands of impoverished Catholic soldiers died in the trenches, having enlisted for a uniform, a wage and ostensible Defence of Small Nations, their 'death gratuities' sent to their families in the slums. Nor were all Irish Protestants automatically Imperialists, as Sean O'Casey joined with 'renegades' of the colonial class, such as W.B. Yeats, Constance Gore-Booth and Maud Gonne, in 'breaking the connection with Britain'. These two women were also prolific painters at the art school.

During her imprisonment after 1916, Constance created propagandist prints of apparently demure Irish women seducing British soldiers for the prison keys. Maud Gonne, subversive daughter of the British garrison, illustrated books of 'Irish peasant ways' as part of her contribution to the Gaelic Revival. Not surprisingly, both women were regarded by their own class as having succumbed to the malaise of 'going native'. Maud Gonne's father was on the HQ Staff of the British Army in Ireland, while Constance fired the opening shots of the revolution, killing a policeman on Stephen's Green, a few hundred yards from the school.

In such a welter of volatile ideologies, as personified by people he knew, and in spite of Kate's concerns, Harry Kernoff could not be immune from the upheavals. These tensions were reflected within the school, as some staff had enlisted for services in the Great War and returned so honoured, while others on their return joined the guerrilla army waging war against British Rule in Ireland.

By and large Harry seems to have skirted the skirmishes on the streets of Dublin and avoided fiery debates among staff and pupils. Kernoff's favourite teacher, Sean Keating, was an ardent Republican, having surrendered a lucrative role as a society painter in London as an apprentice to Orpen, and decided he was not going to 'fight a British War', as he defined 1914-18, and returned to 'be with my own people'. Orpen, though no less Irish, remained to become an official War Artist in London, venturing into the trenches from where his paintings immortalised Empire soldiers cut down in mass butchery. The war experience elevated Orpen to the front rank of world artists as he depicted troops gone mad with trauma, while his eventual expression of the carnage, the *Tomb of the Unknown Soldier*, spoke to – and for – millions of families across Europe.

As Keating held Orpen in high regard, placing him above all living painters, he maintained contact with his one-time tutor and persuaded him to continue his intermittent teaching of portraiture at the school in Dublin. The sundering between Master and Pupil was political not personal. That art could both reflect – and survive – political differences was not lost upon Keating, whose paintings of the War of Independence showed 'the patrician

Self-Portrait in Uniform,
William Orpen, 1917

people of the island engaged in forging their own destiny'. In time the pupil Kernoff, recipient of these lessons, would show the political influences of both these masters.

Patrick Tuohy, a teacher at the school, had been among the armed garrison at the GPO in Dublin which declared aspirant nationhood by force of arms. A gifted painter, whose sombre portraits reflected his own depressive temperament, Tuohy fled to Spain to escape jail and would make his career outside of the country. Other revolutionary-minded students did not survive. Among those who did not return after Easter 1916 was sculptor Willie Pearse, who faced a firing squad dressed in Gaelic garb as a statement of his adopted nationality.

Among other armed activists in Kernoff's class, Maurice Mac-Gonigal managed to deftly wield gun and brush and survive as both guerrilla fighter and painter, his later allegiance becoming wholly artistic. Having entered in the school rolls as Maurice

MacGonigal, after the Revolution he signed his paintings with the Gaelic form of his name, Muiris MacGonigal.

Before the Revolution, Gaelic names were banned by the Metropolitan as stipulated by the centre of arts teaching in South Kensington, London. During Kernoff's early years at the school Keating signed as John Keating while after Independence his signature became Sean Keating, or in Gaelic as 'Ceitin' or simply 'Keating'.

Early on, through the influence of Keating and the haranguing nationalism of MacGonigal, the migrant Jew from London sided with the 'Irish' element in the school, though adroitly adept in public, owing to strictures of his mother. Recalled by contemporaries as taciturn during discussions on politics, one has to remember that in 1920 he was only six years in the country and would not have the overt race memory of his contemporaries. But he certainly had a fugitive race memory which would find due expression in his art.

3

Overcoming Adversity –
The Taylor Prize

Harry Kernoff had other obstacles to surmount. The school was heavily patronised by women students from landed families who lived in their own milieu and could draw on family wealth to sustain their pre-marriage days at the Metropolitan. According to one such, Harry was 'not important', while another female student, Hilda van Stockum, remembers him walking her home in the evening, 'but not given to conversation'. We can surmise that the watchful Kate registered social slights on behalf of her son, though he was not inclined to be communicative or to complain about his personal life.

One presumes he felt apart – and was so regarded – by most other students because of his Russian origin. He was an unknown quantity from their point of view, as – whatever their class differences – all were bound-up in a splintering Irishness, in varying degrees of expression. It was a cliché of the times that the Anglo-Irish, in spite of their political loyalties, were in Britain regarded as 'so very Irish', while at home being demeaned as 'West Brits'. But Harry Kernoff could not be anything but Jewish and 'foreign'.

7/2186238.

By early 1920s, with years of tuition under his belt, Harry was still expected to deliver a full day's work at the family cabinet-making firm. Evening classes were attended mainly by males, as women students with private income formed the bulk of day students and did no manual work, apart from horse grooming and gardening. Unless from a moneyed background, male students had to work during daylight hours to support their studies and only the dedicated handful would then attend classes for two hours, five evenings a week. Harry was in that latter category, doing a full day in his father's workshop and, after an evening meal laid out by Kate, hurrying to evening classes.

The predominance of wealthy women students annoyed Keating, then setting much of the school curriculum. He was not of their class and took umbrage at chatter which discussed servants and social events. Given the volatile times, it was a commentary upon the character and restraint of students and teachers that so much was accomplished. From Kernoff's point of view, being an evening student had its limitations, as tutors were tired from the day's teaching or from their own painting, or were distracted by pressing political interests.

Additionally, the Great War had depleted the teaching staff while those returned faced personal danger peculiar to Ireland in the aftermath of three conflicts – Great War, Rebellion in Ireland and the brutal Civil War. By the 1920s some surviving teachers were absent for weeks at a time, as a matter of life and death. It must have been a hothouse of intrigue and unease, as teachers and students who survived active service in the Great War returned to academic life riven with anxiety that onetime colleagues were conspiring to kill them...

Even so, teaching persisted during academic year from October to July, with an annual fee of fourteen shillings for the less well-off, working out at about a shilling for a week's tuition. After

a day's work in the family workshop, Harry walked from South Circular Road to Kildare Street, past the trams and cabbies and military, to his student place in the lofty rooms of the art school.

It was not all work, of course. Even during political upheaval, students maintained their devotion to pranks, 'masquerades' (fancy dress) and social outings. Harry was unable to partake in many of these, being still bound to his father's business. He balanced the role of dutiful son to the wage-earning father during the day, while surrendering evenings to study and bringing home selective tales of school life to his mother.

One presumes Kate Kernoff was aware of the social nuances of her life in Dublin and her sons' entry into its artistic life. According to other Jewish families in the neighbourhood, she took a keen interest in both her sons' activities, but Harry in particular aroused her vigilance. When sister Lina complained of favouritism, Kate said: 'To whom most is needed, most must be given.' When he stayed out late, as would any young male on the cusp of adulthood, he would find 'De Mammy' sitting in the bay window of Stamer Street, anxiously awaiting his return.

As mentioned, most day students came from well-off backgrounds and had private monies. In the social climate of Anglo-Ireland, which persisted after the Revolution, girls who displayed artistic talent could be admitted to the Metropolitan through family connections, whereas men, on the whole, attended to develop basic drawing skills which would earn them a living as teachers.

This imbalance provoked further ire in John Keating towards the education policies of the new Free State, stumbling as it did out of the sputtering embers of the Revolution. He reminded politicians that it was a state which had been born in promises – but increasingly appeared under the thumbscrew of priests and shopkeepers. He was not given to diplomacy.

In a formal Memorandum to the new Government, Keating asserted that the school was 'in rapid decay', because of the (new) State's grudging attitude to Art and the inherited prevalence of privileged women who:

> ... attended with servants, spend much of the day on telephone calls and absent themselves when they please, go in and out of every room at every hour of day. The young ladies spend their time harmlessly in making little drawings for fashion papers, dresses for fancy dress balls ... give an air of pleasant pettiness to the place...

He excepted 'a few serious students' who:

> ... work in holes and corners ... keen students who hurried home from labouring or office work ... swallowed a hasty tea and rushed to The School for 7 O'Clock ... these young men have ambition, talent and will to learn...

Clearly, Keating had in mind Kernoff and a few others who pursued studies in spite of political violence and personal penury. In return, Kernoff trusted Keating's teaching, especially in techniques of portraiture and drawing of the human figure.

Dublin attacks upon the Jewish Quarter in 1923 revived latent fears for the Kernoffs. In October, a Jewish man was shot on Stephen's Green and the following month, Emanuel Kahn, returning from the Jewish Social Club, was shot dead in Stamer Street, near the Kernoff home. As it happened, one of the Kahn family was an artist and, in common with other families in the district, the Kernoffs felt tribal fear, as the rampant Catholicism of the new Irish government seemed to condone attacks upon Jews.

The police enquiries were laggardly, as the Irish Free State made Roman Catholicism an official religion intolerant of other minority beliefs. The Jewish community was unsettled by the murders and saw Southern Ireland following the path of Catholic powers in Europe, where to be Jewish was to be victimised. Some families left for Manchester, but maintained contact by post, as others went to New York. In spite of that exodus, however, the Kernoff family stayed in Dublin and Harry persisted with his artistic endeavour, which was significantly rewarded in March 1923.

The Taylor Bequest was the most prestigious of awards for emerging talent and consequently was keenly contested by students. The premier award of a Scholarship was won by Harry Kernoff for a watercolour titled *Morning in Dublin*. Apart from the distinction of winning in two categories, watercolour and oils, the latter for *At the Railway Station*, he was the first evening stu-

Winner of the Taylor Prize, At the Railway Station, 1923 – the judges praised the 23-year-old student in perspective, composition and detail

Portrait of Kay 'Hymie',
Harry's brother, 1925

dent to win the Taylor Prize. *At the Railway Station,* one of London's great terminuses, demonstrates a confident blending of architectural perspective with human figures, the striking-looking woman probably his mother, and the little woman behind likely a grandmother. A hasty reprise of the Judge's rules later deprived him of the oil category, on the grounds that a scholarship awardee could not sweep the boards.

The scholarship, however, provided him with free tuition for his final year and £50 in cash, as much as a labourer earned in a year. It was much welcomed at home, where his father worked to sustain two sons, Hymie by now having abandoned art for the retail trade. Kate used the prize moneys for Harry to visit galleries abroad, as the stipulated usage of the prize. He went to London and Paris, visited galleries, studied contemporary paintings in dealers' windows around Bond Street and – he later implied – had sexual 'encounters in Paris', par for the course.

We can surmise Kate did not hear of those episodes, though relatives were appraised of Harry's success, including the public exhibition of his winning entry at the RDS. Usually the Taylor awards were hung in the open spaces of the winning school, but as the school was in the complex which housed the new State's parliament in Kildare Street, the entire area was protected by the military and the public could not enter except under suspicion. So it was to the precincts of the Royal Dublin Society in Ballsbridge that the Kernoff family came to view his winning efforts.

Such distinctions gave him enhanced status in the school and in the wider artistic community, as previous recipients included Orpen, Keating and Tuohy. Keating had won the prize nine years before Harry entered the school, while all owed a debt to Orpen and the tuition he bequeathed of working towards 'the rapport of intimacy with the viewer'.

Keating left a more immediate mark with Harry, who recalled him dangling a skeleton, to emphasise the anatomy of the human figure:

> Don't forget your skeleton, when you draw the surface ... remind yourselves of the muscles under the skin and what makes the visage and frame you are trying to draw.

Keating's concentrated calm while working also appealed to Kernoff, whose own temperament was taciturn. Being in such company, inheriting such standards, destined him for some kind of greatness, yet undefined. Though self-effacing, Harry told a friend that winning was more important than joining the Royal Hibernian Academy, the organisation to whose membership full-time painters aspired.

The scholarship promoted him to Day Student for his final years, with all fees paid, marked in the School Roll of that year as 'Free'. His friend MacGonigal, whose revolutionary activities cut into his artistic output, became a Teacher-in-Training, which guaranteed a salary, as subsidy for the hazards of painting as a career. Harry might have wished for some similar teaching subvention, but with no offer forthcoming, and after discussion at home, he embarked upon a full-time career as an artist.

As he later said, 'I owe a great deal to my mother – my father helped too, as far as he could – to obtain my footing as an artist.' His public thanks was a recognition of Kate's ambitions for her son while recognising his father's role as breadwinner in shaping Harry's destiny.

Embarking on a full-time job as an artist was a risky venture, as uncertain as the foundations of the new State tackling new realities in the wake of a civil war whose brutalities shocked those battling for control of the country. The new government, born out of that conflict, was financially sustained by its former Imperial Ruler and internally by a fragile army and police force, with matters more pressing than promotion of the arts on its agenda. In such an uncertain state, in every sense, official monies were not assigned to 'frivolous pursuits' – Kernoff would have to scrounge as best he could for commissions and patronage. But then, as he said later, 'Being an Artist was all I wanted to be ... from the earliest age.'

4

Dublin Life

Since the elections in 1919, setting up the First Dáil, successive parliaments had been threatened by the sundering of the revolutionaries who had joined in arms three years before to bring about that parliament – but could not agree in its shape or jurisdiction. By 1924, two years into an elected parliament which the majority supported, the stability of the country remained uncertain.

The various parliaments had tried to mesh law-and-order to restore civic life. Most of the heavy industry lay within the Ulster region, likely to separate from the South, which managed to keep going with financial subventions from the British Government and supplies of weapons and munitions, all part of the peace settlement.

In spite of revolutionary promises to 'break the connection', the newly recruited army, police and Civil Service were still heavily dependent upon the goodwill of the former ruler as the native class which took over was not familiar with the levers of power. In the Civil Service, for example, newly-appointed heads of departments routinely conferred by telephone with their former superiors who had re-located to Britain as part of the peace settlement.

It was impossible to make the new state work without the support of Britain and the iron determination of the new Irish governments to resist republican gangs, known as 'die-hards', who continued slash-and-burn attacks upon state institutions. On several occasions, it seemed the fledgling Free State would collapse into the anarchy that had marked its creation. Railways were attacked, locomotives blown-up, bridges and roads mined, public servants of the new state attacked.

In the arts world, given to value judgements of a different kind, the transition was as fraught, though not as physically violent. Writers of such later stature as James Joyce and Sean O'Casey questioned if the revolution had been worth the suffering inflicted by 'the dogs of war'. O'Casey, born into Dublin slums, saw no return for the poor of his city and was harassed when his plays satirised the revolutionaries. Joyce was confirmed in his scepticism when his wife and child, on a visit to Galway, threw themselves to the floor of a railway carriage as it was raked by Republican gunfire.

As for Harry Kernoff, engaged in his own struggle to make a living in unstable times, probably his best mentor at this time was Sean Keating who went out of his way to provide patronage, thereby continuing that support which Orpen had given him while a student. Keating's artistic take on the new political realities provided guidance to the young Jewish aspirant in negotiating a country not his own. Harry had benefited from Keating's interest, helping him at work in his studio during the conflict, where *The Men of the South* had been completed. This seminal painting glorified revolutionary zeal, similar to the verdict of W.B. Yeats that, in spite of barbarities, 'A terrible beauty was born'. In what form 'beauty' might survive in an independent Irish state would elude, with rare exceptions, politicians, poets and artists for generations to come. In Harry's case, it would be expressed with less sentimen-

The Men of the South, Sean Keating, 1921

tality than many of his colleagues, and with more adherence to the pressed-down lives of ordinary people.

By the mid-1920s – and in contrast to Harry's fortunes – artistic purveyors of the 'glory' of the revolution were officially thanked. Yeats was made a Senator in the Upper House of the parliaments (Oireachtas) while Sean Keating received lucrative commissions from state enterprises and on his own recorded a German-built electricity plant harnessing energy by diverting water from the Shannon to drive turbines. Curiously, *The Ardnacrusha* series bears striking similarity to Kernoff's familiarity with Soviet paintings of similar state endeavours on a larger scale, also in the 1920s.

Not that maverick Keating was 'bought', though he used the subvented time to create a searing commentary on the new state that was both paying his way as a teacher and, as he saw it, abandoning socialist ideals of the revolution. *Allegory* depicts a colonial mansion as the roofless symbol of Imperial power, sacked by IRA-men, one of whom is dying to the compliance of priest and politician about to take control from the dispensable guerrilla fighter.

Allegory, Sean Keating, 1922

With this work, Keating signalled his unwillingness to determine how 'Irish Art' would be a plaything of the war-winners, that is, the new Free State. From this distance, the results of the attempts appear whimsical, though at the time they were taken very seriously.

MacGonigal and Keating extolled the 'Spirit of the Gael', romanticising hardy men and 'colleen' women in Connemara and the Aran Islands, providing their versions of 'noble savage' which Jack Yeats had already templated as a counter to the Imperial icons of Turner and Constable. Other painters provided portraits of former IRA gunmen, by now legends in their own afternoons and seen as strutting icons of the new Free State.

No longer a believer in revolutionary promises, Keating was energised by the 'monumentality of the people', looking to the light of the West to illuminate his hard-working small farmers. His personal adoption of their attire, notably the *crios* (belt) and *bainin* (sweater) became a dress code for his political views, later to become a kitsch version of 'Irishness'. Other painters, not tribally identifying with synthetic Gaelic culture as it was hastily imposed, experimented with Modernism – notably Cubism in the case of Mainie Jellett, whose shapes and colours were abstracted from human figures. 'Geometric and circular, with internal symbolism' was one puzzling description of her works which enthused some.

'We sought inner principles and not outer appearance,' she said of her techniques and that of fellow traveller Evie Hone, the latter descended from two centuries of painters. As independent women, they provided the strongest artistic alternative to the newly-risen 'Connemara Culture' of their male peers.

Where did that leave Kernoff? During the mid-1920s he secured paid graphic work for Free State propaganda to mark the transition from 'British' culture to an Irish version. Much was made of artefacts such as the Tara Brooch to demonstrate a 'unique' artistic civilisation claimed to have been suppressed by colonialism, though similar artefacts were commonly found in France and North Africa.

Owing more to prehistoric migrations before 'Irishness' became branded, they were seized upon by an emergent diktat to promote symbols separate from the Imperial panoply of crowns and sceptres. However, in practical matters of day-to-day living, the population was dependent on sterling currency with monarchial insignia, post boxes franked with crown and sceptre, railway station masters in top hats. For his compromise, Kernoff whimsically weaved Jewish and Celtic graphics into insignia for Free State propaganda. Asked about his own nationality, he replied, 'Part Russian, part Spanish, though mostly Irish' – an answer which satisfied officialdom in dispensing commissions.

Quite what defined 'Irish Culture' became as intellectually combustible as the recent civil war had been physically. In America, the revenge of refugees from landlordism hosted exhibitions of a 'Free Ireland' but were indignant at vistas of mountain ranges which could be in Scotland or Wales. In Britain, by contrast, there was a welcome among establishment patrons for visuals of the 'noble peasantry' as expressed by Jack Yeats, Sean Keating and Paul Henry.

In literature, Sean O'Casey depicted the urban peasantry as hostile to Independence which had ground them into deeper poverty. 'It's not the gunmen who are dying for the people, it's the people who are dying for the gunmen' was a riposte that offended official sensitivities, as did the character of Rosie Redmond's young prostitute plying the oldest profession in a new Catholic state. In the streets and pubs there was much risibility for the promotion of an alternative female ideal. 'Mother Ireland, you're rearing them yet' – a common response to lectures on purity from clerics claiming celibacy.

As the 'colleen' promoted by Keating – strong-faced, shawled and handsome – was adopted as the female ideal of the Saorstat Éireann, what it meant in practice was left to the penalties of the confessional during Catholic crusades.

Amusingly, the official Irish version of sainted Irish womanhood was modelled on Hazel Lavery, wife of the painter Sir John Lavery. A free-thinking American of wealth, Lady Lavery had hosted a political salon during the London negotiations leading to the Free State and held in emotional thrall – some say sexual as well – Michael Collins and Kevin O'Higgins, both revolutionary leaders. After the death of Collins, her portrait was imprinted onto the new Irish pound note to replace the King as the salon siren of Kensington rose from her chaise longue and swapped her 'flapper' dress for a Connemara shawl.

By then, O'Casey had left Dublin, in the wash of Joyce's departure, each citing survival. Joyce's magisterial 'to forge ... the uncreated conscience of my race' was matched by O'Casey's diatribes

The Irish pound note, featuring Lady Lavery

against Church and Free State. For those aspirants left to cope, the dilemmas were pressing, given the penury of many artists. As Liam O'Flaherty said to Harry during a debate at the Radical Club: 'I've had enough talk about the soul of Ireland! Give me a bit more hospitals, schools and decent roads.'

O'Flaherty's verdict was of 'foolish parochial nationalism and bigotry'. Having been shell-shocked during the Great War, in his recovery wanderings in Europe he had evolved a radical view of politics. Kernoff's instincts attracted O'Flaherty who encouraged him to become an early member the Studio Arts Club.

The two struck up a friendship, marked by O'Flaherty's interest in Kernoff's inherited Communism – and his declared sympathies for the poor – which did not sit well with the arts establishment. The Studio Arts Club attracted younger painters alienated by the academic tradition of the RHA whose approval was a route to financial commissions. 'Hanging Committees' which promoted new artists were usually packed by painters in the academic tradition and thereby hostile to Modernism.

Alternatives as offered by the O'Flaherty brothers, Liam and Tom – who had seen more European painting than the RHA judging panel – encouraged other artists to find a willing support-er in Kernoff. The venue was Daniel Egan's Salon, run by a former student of the Metropolitan School, who, because of the looting during the Revolution, had abandoned studies in order to salvage the family business. Egan's Salon in Stephen's Green held a stock of continental Old Masters and hosted younger painters. Billed as the Radical Club, during 1926 it featured Kernoff, MacGonigal, Keating, Nano Reid and Paul Henry and attracted a sizeable turn-out of enthusiasts.

Harry Kernoff outdid both his teachers in supplying twelve works, including a bronze head of his brother, Kay. Paul Henry, seen as radical with his 'low horizon' and tumbling clouds above land and water bereft of people, was clearly affected by Van Gogh's landscapes, which he had seen in Paris. Henry's paintings of sparsely-populated coastal vistas were in tune with the romantic notions of urban Irish sentimentalists.

Henry was also included in another grouping, along with Jack B. Yeats, called Dublin Painters' Society, again in reaction to the

Old Mill Portmarnock, c. 1926

RHA. By now a predictable joiner of new movements, Kernoff was among the coteries who exhibited in small galleries.

While participating in these fringe movements, he nonetheless set his primary sights on the RHA. In debates about Modernism, he was adroit, preferring to keep his paint dry for commissions that would free him from his father's business. Though the Taylor Prize relieved Isaac of paying final year school fees, Harry was still expected to pay his way at home by delivering hours in the workshop. Embarking on a full-time career as an artist was clearly hazardous during the civic and economic chaos of the late 1920s.

By then, Kate had moved the family to No. 13 Stamer Street, where Harry painted in the attic, with a spill of light and a commanding view of the laneways to the rear of the house where he observed the coming and going of Dubliners in their daily tasks.

By the standards of the time, No. 13 was a substantial Victorian two-storey over basement, with granite steps to the porch and elegant plaster work in the living rooms. The Mezuzah of the Diaspora, a scroll inside a metal case, was formally installed in the right portal of the hall door. With the purchase of this commanding residence and gardens, the Kernoffs arrived as people of substance in the community of the South Circular Road. One might surmise the move was mainly due to his mother being credited with making the major family decisions.

As for her eldest son, Kate encouraged the Jewish community to help with modest commissions. As a diasporic settlement in Dublin, it had tentacles at many levels of business and also conducted welfare; meeting co-religionists at ports, some of whom spoke little English, induction at synagogues which organised schooling for children and functions for elders. The community's strength was measured by its willingness to help Jewish people 'hatch, match and despatch', and in between bankrolling new entrants to business.

No. 13 Stamer Street, Dublin 8 – the family home during Harry's lifetime

There were good reasons for cohesion. Anti-Semitism had been rife in Europe since the middle ages and rampant in the latter part of the nineteenth century, with hundreds of pogroms upon Jews in Christian countries. Ireland was no exception, as in Kernoff's time Jews were stoned out of Limerick after a sermon by a priest, and in Dublin Jews were barred from leading golf and athletic clubs, from some professional societies, and were frequently the butt of comment in newspapers from the newly empowered Catholic middle classes.

The new Catholic State did not easily assimilate difference, but neither did the Jewish establishment, whose prevailing drive was to better itself materially, while offering a marginalised living to its artists. In time, Kernoff would relate more to the wider Irish population and less to his racial origins.

5

O'Flaherty, 'Toto' and Cabaret

I f political confusion and economic chaos was in the Dublin air of the 1920s, political cabaret thrived. Several small theatres provided evening entertainment, with lyrics adapted to domestic issues. Usually housed in basements, these venues had input from what migrants had seen abroad.

The O'Flaherty brothers, promoting political cabaret, asked for material performed against painted sets by Harry Kernoff, whose efforts were usually described as 'realistic' by newspaper critics not conversant with theatre outside of Ireland. Church and state looked with disfavour on these small efforts. The state was promoting 'Irishness' though a national radio station, '2RN', which broadcast government policies and a musical fare of ballads.

In that flotsam it was hardly surprising that various émigrés, transplanted by the Great War, would find new identities. When Harry met Madame 'Toto' Bannard-Cogley – a dramatic-looking woman of French upbringing – the attraction was strong. 'Toto', as she was known, made much of her revolutionary past, as she and her journalist husband had transmitted the Irish insurgents' versions of events to European newspapers, often at variance with the official British account. After the Treaty, as state agencies took over propaganda, wartime excitement settled to a calmer life and

Kernoff's Madame 'Toto' Cogley, 1930

Madame Toto was not alone in looking to replace the heady revolutionary times with avant garde theatre.

In ramshackle 1920s Dublin she found a scene suitable to her talents, organising cabaret shows and recruiting from the standing army of 'would-be geniuses, boulevardiers and tosspots'.

It took more than layabouts to get a theatre going. Her capacity to organise – and cajole – attracted artists alienated by the 'offeechal' Abbey Theatre, now under diktat of W.B. Yeats and Lady Gregory for whom Fairies, Fantasies and Peasant Drama seemed the desired fare. To Madame Toto came writers Denis Johnston and Liam O'Flaherty, actress Coralie Carmichael, Tom Casement (brother of the executed Roger Casement) and later a couple of travelling actors, Hilton Edwards and Michael MacLiammoir. All mucked in, one way and another, to make theatre in a wooden shed at No. 41 Harcourt Street.

Harry Kernoff's contribution ranged from set construction to scene-painting, notably a collage of heads of the theatre's founders, cast as refugees aboard a Noah's Ark, fleeing the floods of Irish bombast. Madame Toto was at the Ark's helm, handsome and defiant, supported by Johnston and other luminaries. Kernoff cast their body shapes as bird and animals reflective of their character. It became a narrative painting as it was updated and extended over the years along the walls of the theatre, whose dramatic fare, not respectful of the new establishment, quickly gathered audiences on Saturday nights.

Theatre sets and scene painting ran parallel with Kernoff's graphic work for Dublin periodicals, which were noted by publishers in London and New York. He was making a name as an artist who would deliver on time, ensuring steady work in a city where many talents were culled by excessive drink.

Through all this activity, and though long graduated from art school, he continued to attend informal classes, where the atmosphere was congenial as MacGonigal and Keating brought news of commissions as their fortunes ebbed and flowed with tides of fashion and commerce. Under such distinguished tutors as the sculptor Oliver Sheppard and stained-glass genius Harry Clarke, Kernoff continued to absorb lessons from the great as shown in his output the 1920s.

A rigorous routine produced paintings from the attic in Stamer Street, alternating with woodcuts which required tensile strength to cut into the material. For all his slight stature, Harry was strong and efficient in cutting. Sometimes he went against the grain, sometimes with it, as he matched portraiture to the character of the wood. Then he would break for lunch with Kate, who was fond of her food and regarded meals as a mandatory family

Nelson's Pillar, GPO, Dublin, 1935 – woodcut

ritual. After lunch he faced into more work on graphic and print-making in the studio.

Some evenings he left Stamer Street to meet friends, their talk lubricated by absinthe, a favoured potent tipple of the Bohemian set, though his tolerance for alcohol was limited. By his late twenties he had attained the life he wished. On any given week, he worked on two or three paintings in the morning, two or three woodblock or lino cuts in the afternoon and any numbers of graphic illustrations. The paintings were usually in watercolour, some for merchant families, often as a follow-up to a supper given by Kate to stalwarts of her community.

Other portraits were cast wider, such as those of Liam O'Flaherty, whom he placed against a skewed Aran island, the writer's birthplace. It was a novel effect for the times, as was his perspective of the Rotunda Hospital, where O'Flaherty had raised the Red Flag during the Revolution, an emblem rare among the two other revolutionary banners of the Citizen Army and Irish Republic. Skewing the perspective could be seen as a mild doff to Modernism, then a talking point among the avant-garde.

For all the experiments, conventional magazine graphics were the bread-and-butter, done in pen and black ink in Stamer Street, then delivered to the printers for block-making. Other light drawings were done in pencil and crayon, sometimes beginning as whimsical doodles for friends. Watercolour was his fastest medium, as he controlled the coursing of the paints with water, adjusting to the tilt of damp paper. His pastel portraits – using watercolour and crayon – became characteristic of his style, with chalk strokes to heighten nose, temple and cheeks.

Woodcuts took longer, requiring a reverse of the image to be cut into wood or linoleum, using knives from his father's workshop.

The woodcuts showed strong, hard straight lines, instinctively more urban than rural. Some were repeat versions of existing paintings in lino or wood and could be a 'good seller'. Such masterful works as *Winetavern Street* and *A Bird*

Portrait of Liam O'Flaherty, 1936

Never Flew on One Wing would be repeated as woodcuts in response to demand – as would the versions of James Connolly of the Citizen Army and poet W.B. Yeats. The lino cut of Sir Roger Casement, for instance, was done from a photograph covertly taken at the trial in London, brought to Ireland by sympathisers, and offered to Kernoff to immortalise a revolutionary idealist.

This puts focus on Kernoff's political sympathies. Given his peer group, from Keating to MacGonigal to O'Flaherty, it's hardly surprising that he was on the left of the political spectrum. Nor was it their influence alone which accounts for a lifelong position on the Republican Left – he already harboured a family view of how politics should respond when the political Right held sway.

This family feeling lay in flight from Russia, when Jews were persecuted by Czarist police, a migration that became syndicalist theories of the 1890s by refugee Jewish activists whose writings laid the analytical structure that became the iron fist of Communism that would mesmerise Europe for successive generations.

Woodcut of Roger Casement, 1936

'Man is born free, but is everywhere in chains' was a mantra that impelled Russian socialists as Kernoff's family settled in London, unknowingly then destined for Ireland. Radicalism may have appeared an unlikely force in his mild manner, but surfaced through public events in Ireland.

At this time, in the 1920s, his emotional involvement was not with the emergent Free State but in theatre, painting and publishing: he did not let

Mother and Child Going Home, 1931 – woodcut

political feelings get in the way of making a living, being glad of paid work from the new establishment, though his political sympathies were with groupings that might be loosely defined as Republican Socialists.

Opposed to creation of the Free State, defeated in a bitter civil war, these underground groupings by the mid-1920s had become more debating shops than a serious threat, monitored by the detective units of the new Civic Guard. From recent opening of State archives, we learn that some of the groups Kernoff associated with received monies from Soviet Russia, though it's unlikely he was personally a beneficiary as his accounting books show modest fees for designs of political pamphlets for the Republican Left.

It is hardly surprising that those detectives took an interest in him or that his masthead of the *Irish Worker* newspaper became a clipping in police files – minor commissions compared to his series of drawings of trade union leaders for *Voice of Irish Labour*, which he signed with initials KN instead of his full name. These showed where his political loyalties lay, but again formed only a tiny part of a prolific output which appeared in magazines and books in Ireland, Britain and America. These ran into hundreds providing regular income, as he evolved towards self-sufficiency as an artist. He laboured in graphics and print to buy time as a painter in oils and watercolours.

The decision by the powerful 'hanging committee' of the RHA to select five of his painting for the 1926 exhibition delivered the right stimulus at the right time.

6

Entry to the RHA, 1926

The Royal Hibernian Academy (RHA) sat comfortably at the top of artistic aspiration, garnishing entries from world-class painters. As Osborne, Orpen, Lavery, Yeats and Keating had benefited from regular exhibitions there, the young artist Harry Kernoff hoped for similar advance after five of his works were chosen for the RHA annual exhibition in 1926. He arrived into the company of two of his benefactors, as that year Jack Yeats showed five works and Keating eight.

Kernoff's were *Autumn Avenue, Phoenix Park, Players in the Park, Portrait of the Artist, The Judgement of Paris* and an *Old Tree, Richmond* – this last a series which he painted on regular visits to London, housed and welcomed by relatives as he wandered afresh with an eye to subjects in the city of his birth. Although not singled out in *The Irish Times* review of the RHA Exhibition – that accolade was reserved for a portrait of George Bernard Shaw – Kernoff was among those praised.

The prestige of the RHA had an effect, as he received commissions for portraits. By the following year he was equipped to submit another selection to the RHA, of which six were accepted. Again he featured in the general praise, but this time commissions were sparse. Harry complained to a friend that he had expected

Phoenix Park, 1928 – watercolour

more in the way of 'filthy lucre'. He fell back upon illustration work, which included Free State propaganda and drawings for American anthologies of Irish writers.

Portraiture was his abiding interest, often providing stimulus when fee-paying magazine work became tedious. On portraits he worked fast, completing the subject in a few sittings, 'in one sitting if possible, as thereby keeping the work fresh for the viewer'.

In spite of the praise garnered from both subjects and viewers, his versions were not received by academic critics as having the depth or character as those of Orpen, Keating or Lavery, with whom he was unfairly compared. Those artists were at the height of their powers and, in the case of Orpen and Lavery, benefited from powerful establishment patronage in Britain.

The emerging Irish establishment had adopted Keating as a 'semi-state artist', whereas for Kernoff and contemporary MacGonigal it was a case of hoping for commissions. MacGonigal received a wage as a teacher at the school, while in Kernoff's case, without his illustrations for magazines and books, he would have been poor. Living at home, subsidised in day-to-day living with Kate providing three full meals a day and feeling slighted if Harry, more than his siblings, was not present for meals legendary in size. In spite of such generous nurturing, her favourite son, being lean, did not put on weight, as on the male side they were a slim, trim species.

He was, anyway, absorbed by the life which Dublin then provided. In spite of the pact between Church and state to limit pleasure and invoke penal obedience, an underground Bohemian set made its own culture, scorning those who made a show of public piety at variance with their private behaviour. The post-revolutionary state also gave a dispensation to those whose money and political influence allowed them to flout conventions. By the late 1920s, for instance, of the hundreds of homosexuals in prison, most were from poor, rural or working-class families, while a 'smart-set', protected by family influence, flaunted their tastes in Dublin's underground bars and cafes.

Some gaelicised their names, such as the actor Michael Mac-Liammoir, while others made a satiric charade of church-going as a career move, as Church and state between them controlled most jobs by way of teachers, police, army and the civil service. In the countryside, the small farming class expanded on the back of seizure from Protestant landlords, with the state purchasing from – and parcelling out – the lands of the former ruling class. Those who resisted were often encouraged to leave by threats to burn out their 'big houses', which the new police force would often ignore. Industries such as brewing, grain and building stayed within the control of the former ruling class, suspicious of the Catholic tide whose avarice washed against their doors.

In the arts world, dominated by freer spirits, Catholics had to tread carefully or risk 'the belt of a crozier' – a public condemnation by a Bishop which threatened livelihood. Because of such

Liberty Hall, Night

sanctions, the so-called Bohemian culture evolved underground. But the arts world was also a great leveller, uniting diverse interests of class, religion and nationality. For all the criticisms levelled at it, the RHA held fast to an academic standard to bestow patronage.

Of the six works delivered for another showing at RHA, *Liberty Hall, Night* was a grey, ghostly rendering of a trade union building which was seminal to the socialist leadership of Connolly and Larkin during the revolution. Other pictures in his second RHA showing were *Sunlight Workshop*, of his father's business; *Behind the Scenes,* from his work as scene-painter and imbued with theatrical irony; *A Labour Meeting* focuses on Jim Larkin, noted for his oratorical resistance to merchant power, addressing a crowd of men whose hats are in angled symmetry to the future; *To the Inevitable* was a rare homage to Abstract Modernism and *Ploughed Fields, Portmarnock*, at first sight a rural scene in traditional style is an exercise in geometric perspective.

A milestone in the professional life of an artist is a first solo exhibition, which Kernoff undertook the following year, in 1928. He was encouraged by Madame Cogley who presided over the venue, the Little Theatre, South William Street, where he generated a lead review from *The Irish Times*:

> [Kernoff] ... sees colour and light without the bias of convention ... as pleasing in rhythm and composition as in their marked impress of personality.

Already registering with critics were his urban scenes, with the reviewer picking out *Charlemont Street Bridge*, and adding praise for the fine night skies and gas-light shadows of two other paintings, *College of Surgeons*, by Stephen's Green, which contained hues of Liberty Hall, and *Tram at Night*, an eerily powerful tram going over Leeson Street Bridge.

Of his portraits, a crucial test of a young painter, *The Irish Times* praised them as being clever and arresting in the flesh tints and shadows. All his work is arresting by reason of its sincerity and original outlook. Other positive reviews confirmed the rightness of the path taken. Though living at home, at aged twenty-eight, he was approaching maturity as a man and as an artist.

Around this time, too, his romantic life flourished, though his Jewishness and his mother's abiding interest meant it would never be simple in terms of marriage and a family of his own.

Tram at Night

7

Of Madame Toto and 'The Boys'

M adame Bannard-Cogley, to give her full title, cut a curve through theatrical life in Dublin during the closing years of the 1920s. She cared not a whit for the new conservatism that imposed censorship of books, plays and films. As seen by historian John Regan: 'The Catholic Church and most politicians were obsessed by the idea of imported evil corrupting native innocence.' Anything 'in general tendency obscene' usually meant sexual activity, while 'a danger to Faith and Morals' meant whatever Catholic censors wanted it to mean.

'Toto' managed to keep the Studio Theatre in business, warding off moral busybodies, cajoling performers, raising funds and moulding a company which offered alternatives to the mainstream Abbey and Gate Theatres. At the Abbey, for instance, after its rejection of Sean O'Casey's *The Silver Tassie* as too modernist, plays were invariably set in a farmhouse kitchen or country road, with actors speaking a strange sing-song that was held to be 'naturalistic' or 'spiritual', reflective of idealised rural life. There was also a penchant for the supernatural. Between the fairies of the poet Yeats and the sing-song of Synge, there was little room for hard-edged political plays which reflected urban life.

Circus and spectacle evaded the censors, in spite of their scrutiny. Dublin's largest theatre, the Royal, had eight tigers and four lions as onstage performers at the beginning of 1928, while elsewhere dancing girls known as 'flappers' ran the gauntlet of the moral brigade. Films were the new draw, with live piano music as soundtrack and dancing courtesan Louise Brooks on screen. Brooks, with her stylish dress and 'Bob' hair cut, became a role model for Madame Cogley. Somewhere around this time, too, she and Kernoff became lovers, a coupling that caused no great frisson among the theatricals, though Toto had a husband and family. As all were engaged in the great enterprise of a new kind of theatre, Kernoff's professional and personal life meshed comfortably.

It was, in many ways, a time of re-invention of self, for those with the flair to make new things. The Free State, less than a decade old, was trying to convince that it was legitimate, to impress upon its population that independence from Empire meant something positive and uplifting, which most of its hapless citizens did not perceive, beyond a change of coinage, flag and increased poverty following wars.

Visually, the transition was cosmetic as incumbent figureheads of the new state mimicked symbols of Imperial office – top hat, long coat and horse carriage – while the new Army retained rank and regalia of the departed British military. Jobs were scarce, unemployment rife, crime rampant and living standards had not improved. The 'intelligentsia' was mainly deluded, drunk or had disappeared, their function as moulders of public opinion largely suppressed by the Roman Catholic Church on a mission to right wrongs going back to Henry VIII.

Two mendicant English actors, Alfred Willmore and Hilton Edwards, delivering Shakespeare to remote towns, were mentioned to Toto by Kernoff's friend, A.J. Leventhal, as keen to start a theatre not bound by nationalist rhetoric. Ostensibly English, both claimed pedigrees from London theatre schools, with Willmore

('The Big Will' in Dublin slang) gaelicising his name to Mac-Liammoir (Son of Big Will).

Kernoff's portrait of Micheal MacLiammoir

Their pedigrees later proved fictional. MacLiammoir claimed Cork as his birthplace, whereas in fact it was Willesden in London, a drab suburb of the lower-middle class. His companion Hilton Edwards had similar creativity about his background, claiming his father to be 'Governor of Hydabrand and Sing' in India. According to the biographer of the pair, Hilton's father, whom the young Edwards hardly knew, was a 'Joint Magistrate (second grade) in Calcutta'.

Such creativity fitted neatly into the flux of the times. There was also the very Irish situation that 'street level' homosexuals and 'rough trade' were regularly jailed, while a dispensation was afforded to public figures in the arts and religion, providing they 'didn't frighten the horses' by displays of their sexuality. As homosexuals in Britain were also subject to jailing, often politically motivated, Southern Ireland provided a bolt hole for those with establishment connections.

That Ireland proved a fertile ground in which the mendicant Son of Big Will and his fugitive companion Edwards might thrive is shown in 'Toto's memoir of their meeting:

> ... at the end of June 1928, I met 'The Boys' as we still call them. They were looking for somewhere to start their theatre and Conty Leventhal had told them to get in touch with me as being someone trying to work on the same lines. The Boys were brought round one Saturday evening by Bulmer Hob-

son. We talked and talked – or rather Hilton talked, Michael punctuated and I glowed with enthusiasm. Before the night was out I knew that my dreams and hopes were realised... I asked them to appear at my cabaret. They agreed and said they'd do a scene from Macbeth. I gave them a decor contrived from two wicker baskets covered with large purple velvet cape – one of my most cherished 'props'. The lighting was most effective, red and blue gelatines over biscuit-boxes. And so were presented for the time together in Dublin the two young men who have since made Theatre History in Dublin and Ireland.

In time, the Gate brought European drama to the capital, as an alternative to the exaltation of peasant fare promoted by the Abbey. For Kernoff as set designer and scene painter, the addition of the Gate facilitated friendships. While not theatrical in his own demeanour, indeed notable for his reticence, he contributed a quiet craft of getting the job done and on time, as his father Isaac had taught him in cabinet-making. But, oddly enough – or perhaps as unconscious rejection of the family trade – the picture frames he made from end pieces discarded in the family workshop were generally poor. 'Terrible' was one verdict. 'Harry seem to use bits of architrave and beading to make frames which never seemed right.' A comment that fitted neatly into the native prejudice about Jewish penny-pinching.

Such trivia aside, his work ethic made him attractive to women, used as they were to flamboyant but unreliable men, often reared by doting mothers and thereby prone to petulance or alcohol when confronted with strong women seeking intimacy. Kernoff, on the other hand, while possessed of a watchful mother at home, was a spry seducer abroad. He stretched himself and was met more than halfway by eager women. According to Ciaran MacGonigal, son of painter Maurice MacGonigal, Kernoff had 'elfin charm with

Miss Fitzgerald, 1931 – one of many female portraits by Harry Kernoff

women and spoke to them on a one-to-one basis, which they liked and found intimacy growing.'

Among those he romanced were the Abbey actresses Sheila Richards and Ria Mooney, whose portraits he painted. Though one imagines the relationships growing amid the chemistry of artist and sitter as often happened in such situations, it's unlikely much physical activity took place in his attic studio, with the Mammy downstairs, alert to extra-artistic endeavour and bringing up cups of tea as strategic interruption.

According to informants of the time, his longer relationship was with 'Toto' Cogley, who inspired a series of paintings over the next few years, as their intimacy became translated, for him, into Muse, Temptress, Goddess and eventually, when passion waned, to Friend. These images of her character as it evolved through his arts is traceable over two decades through direct portraits and her influence on his set pieces – her striking eyes and long jawbone were borrowed by him for other subjects, often theatrical or mythic, such as *Byzantine Madonna* and *Celtic Warrior*.

Apart from designing sets and 'decor' as it was known, work in theatre provided outlets denied many Jewish men, who were constricted within a community aware of its difference in custom and religion. Jewish men were expected to choose partners – and eventually marry – from within the tribe – an expectation

Merchant's Arch, Temple Bar, Dublin 2 – the artist is seen crossing the Ha'peny Bridge with his trademark valise of artists' materials.

Egans General Store, Tullamore, County Offaly – watercolour over pencil, probably a commission by the store owners, though the artist has slipped in a drinker and lounger and one of his trademark 'rumpy' women for context.

Ancient mariner in Ringsend.

Madonna with Fawn and Doves – cabaret artis Toto Cogley was Harry's muse for a variety of wo

Tram over Leeson Street Bridge – the male figure on the left is likely the painter Jack B. Yeats who lived nearby.

St. Stephen's Green – Harry was a regular observer in Stephen's Green, resulting in dozens of views of this Dublin park.

Costumes for theatre – during the 1920s/1930s Harry designed masquerades and plays at various Dublin theatres, notably the Gate and Abbey.

*James Joyce – pastel and chalk on card, sitting arranged by A. J. Leventhal,
a friend of Joyce who asked Kernoff if any Blooms were living in Dublin.*

A Bird Never Flew on One Wing, Or Alcoholics Synonymous – this well known work has a montage of pub names and a cavalier pair of drinkers, Fat Man and Thin Man, the latter becoming the model for Mr Spock in the TV series Star Trek.

Watercolur of Custom House Dock, viewed by the Ancient Mariner from the North Quay.

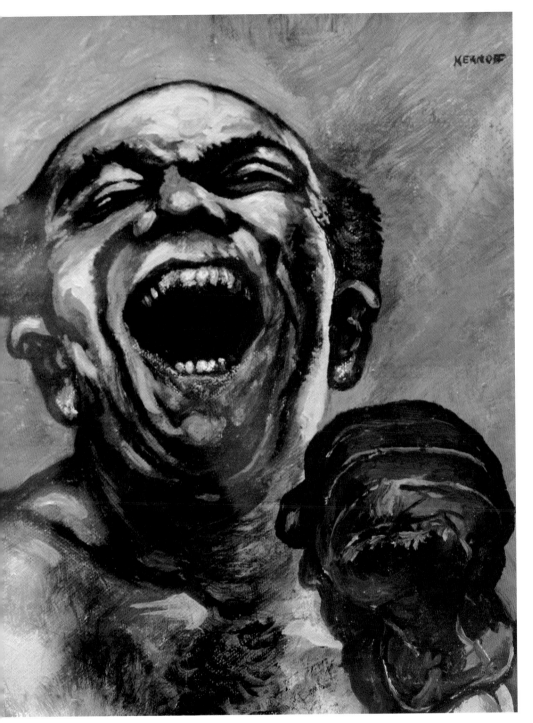

'It's a Knockout!' – the full vigour of contest, oil on board, c. 1950s.

*Delia Murphy, famous ballad singer and wife of a diplomat,
whom Harry Kernoff 'romanced' for about twenty years.*

so strong that a minority who found it constricting left Ireland for wider choices.

Britain, America and South Africa were the countries favoured by eligible young men, while young women mainly went to Manchester and Glasgow a few times a year to attend social events designed to find them husbands. Against that kind of tribal enforcement, Dublin theatres provided Harry Kernoff with possibilities beyond those of his co-religionists, in the variety of work and in romantic encounters which did not carry the expectation of marriage. Theatre also gave him patterns of socialising as a relief from the rigorous studio work in Stamer Street, where leading personalities from politics and the arts sat for portraits alongside humbler denizens of Dublin life. As mentioned, one sitting was favoured by him, because 'the paint flows and image is fresh thereby. One imagines, too, he encouraged his subjects to talk as a means of gleaning character, though taciturn himself in response. As with much else in his life, the work came first.

8

Joyce, Jewishness and Dublin ...

When James Joyce published *Ulysses* in 1922, the fields of Europe were still manuring dead from 1914-18. In time, T.S. Eliot's *The Waste Land* invoked the despair of ordinary people at the mass slaughter inflicted by their rulers upon their subjects. For most people in Ireland, recovering from the convulsions of their Civil War, the publication in Paris of a 'bewk' by a Dubliner did not register.

In his native city, a mere smattering knew of *Ulysses*, and of those a smaller number managed to wade through the multi-layered meanderings of its characters. Puzzlement was the primary reaction, even to some who featured. As the book assumed iconic weight abroad and scholars beat a path to its Dublin door, the native coterie struggled to understand. A keeper of the National Library denied a suggestion that he was a character in *Ulysses* – no he was actually himself, doing his job as a keeper of books. In the village of Dublin, Joyce was cut down with a tawdry: 'Ah jays, yeah I knew him well – well not himself, but his oul' fella, say ... ah jays ...'.

Joyce's father, whose many colourful phrases were transposed to the book, was indeed well known as a character, with a 'promising future behind him' and 'a praiser of his own past'. As habitué of pub and brothel, he had been painted by Patrick Tuohy,

58

a tutor at the art school who had taught Kernoff. The artist now registered the Dublin meandering of another Jew, Bloom. From A.J. Leventhal, he received accounts of the author's settlement in Paris. Joyce asked Leventhal if any with the Bloom name were left in Dublin and was told no. Joyce was wary of possible legal reaction, as the manuscript of *Dubliners* had been refused by local printers on the grounds that 'fictional' characters were identifiable from their pub habitat.

Pencil sketch of an ill James Joyce

Through these Dublin connections Joyce agreed to sit for a sketch by Kernoff, helped by mention of Patrick Tuohy's portrait of the writer's father. Kernoff's pencil sketch was afterwards completed as a pastel of watercolour, crayon and chalk (see first section of colour plates). It shows an introspective, bemused Joyce a few years after the publication of his epic, still subject to the 'agenbite of inwit' that affects his characters. As *Ulysses* impacted belatedly upon an Irish public, Kernoff sourced other characters from the book in a personal odyssey that imitated Bloom's.

These perambulations over many years resulted in dozens of portraits, notably the Toucher Doyle as caught in all his staged beggaring, while John Boyle Pierse O'Reilly carries the innate flamboyance of a walk-on part in what would become the book of the century. As for Kernoff, long after *Ulysses* had become

Davy Byrnes 'moral pub' in Dublin's Duke Street, made famous in **Ulysses**, *as seen by Kernoff from the Bailey pub opposite.*

globally famous, he continued to find in its pages characters, settings and the urban habitat he knew intimately.

Among the painter's many parallel lives, putting onto board locations associated with Joyce became an artistic odyssey of his own, marked emotionally by the second portrait of James Joyce, completed shortly after the outbreak of the Second World War in which the author of the mammoth novel looks despairingly ill from the stomach ulcer that would kill him.

9

The 1930s – Effects of the Russian Experience

Though the 1930s was a dreadful time for European Jews, Kernoff relieved the prevailing mood by work and periodic bouts of travel. While his work ethic produced a rigorous schedule, it also helped evade the debates about Modernism, an artistic reflection of the fracturing of nation states in war. Though not averse to experimentation, his method was by his thirties largely classical – yet within that tradition, his palette differed from his contemporaries. As one critic assessed in 1928:

> Mr Kernoff is no longer a mere decorative painter, not yet an experimenter with Cubism. Several portraits, landscapes and genre ... display originality of conception ... a critic's puzzlement at an Irish-domiciled artist not painting in the traditions of Ireland or Britain.

While his *At the Railway Station*, which had featured in the Taylor Prize, came in again for praise, *The Irish Times* reviewer singled out *Dogma* as:

> ... brave work of allegory; a female figure chained with the world splitting at her feet ... her victims are revolution, war,

death and deceit and treachery ... the whole in a blue scheme
of colour, with darker purples expressive of the psychology of
the picture.

Even the term 'psychology' in a review was fairly advanced for
the time and unwittingly showed how he had touched into the
beat of Europe, while his contemporaries were immersed in Celtic
fantasies as an unconscious buffer to the outside world. As Depression took hold in North America, Britain was also caught by
internal unrest provoked by the economic downturn. The social
order of many European countries broke under the strain of mass
poverty and hunger marches. Continental Europe plunged into
economic chaos, exploited by the Nazis as a prelude to a further
outbreak of mass murder.

Long before the world knew of genocide against Jews, the
Kernoff family in Dublin heard of the war against their race, as
enacted in Germany, Austria, France, Belgium and Holland. It
seemed to his family that flight from war marked their own narrative – from Russia at the end of the nineteenth century to England
and from England to Ireland to escape the Great War. But now, as
war sounded again during the 1930s, one vast territory was apparently standing for peace and resisting mass murder of its citizens.

As the political Left saw it, Russia provided an example of
how states should both protect their citizens internally and stand
against external threats. *Mir* – peace – was a watchword after the
Russian Revolution, whose tenets promised deliverance from poverty and servitude. As Russia in theory demolished Czardom and
class privileges that flowed from monarchy, the communist remit
expanded to Asian and European states in what became human-
kind's largest mass experiment in social order. The means of production were taken over by the workers – in theory. In fact, as
became known later, the means of production were controlled by

Soviet apparatchiks who, in order to maintain their power, visited famine, civil war and murder upon mainly illiterate populations.

This betrayal of ideals since the heady days of 1917 was largely unknown to the naive Irish group which set out to visit the Soviet Union during 1930. Styling themselves Friends of Soviet Russia, they denied the growing terror as evidence of a failure of 1917 – their ideological belief dismissed such reports as 'lies of the capitalist press'. Drawing parallel with failure, post-1916, to bring about ideals of that revolution, Irish Friends of Soviet Russia clung to Communism as an antidote to Irish disillusion.

Not surprisingly, the group was regarded as subversives by the new Irish establishment. Among the Friends of Soviet Russia who voyaged were Hannah Sheehy-Skeffington, a revolutionary whose pacifist husband had been shot in 1916, Maud Gonne McBride, object of 'heart's desire' of W.B. Yeats, and Charlotte Despard, feminist and suffragette.

Kernoff's interest was different. Though sympathetic to his fellow-travellers, he was more interested in Russian art and state support for artists. The group's main interest was to see how a post-revolutionary state solved the formidable problems of housing, literacy and education. How, in effect, did it free from poverty the people it claimed to have liberated?

On the voyage, Hanna Sheehy-Skeffington lost little time making the acquaintance

Woodcut of James Connolly, 1935

of the Captain, and organised a presentation by Harry, whom she called 'our artist delegate', of his woodcut of James Connolly. In a speech, which Harry translated, she defined Connolly as:

> The Irish Revolutionary Leader who was executed after the Easter Rising in Dublin, May 4th 1916 ... a signatory to the Proclamation who gave his life to set up an Irish Workers' Republic.

She cited his political mantra:

> 'I cannot conceive of a Free Ireland with a subject working class and cannot conceive of a free working class in a subject Ireland.'

Her enthusiasm for everything Russian impressed the Captain, though privately Sheehy-Skeffington thought the food crude, was amused at eggs served in glasses, tea without milk and indigestible cuts of gristle meat. On arrival, she was even more disposed to being impressed by the tour guides, unaware they were carefully selected to impart the official doctrine.

Discouraged from making formal notes, she covertly wrote on flimsy paper of 'Russian women ... freed from pots and pans and household slavery', without revealing to whom fell the drudgery of housekeeping. Obvious shortages of foods she justified because 'no cafes served to abolish samples of privilege'. She had been advised to leave her umbrella behind, as it was a symbol of bourgeoisie dress, but missed it, as she habitually carried one. As a woman usually well turned out, with a flair for hats, she became self-conscious of her own fashionable dress, feeling Russians saw her as 'a bourgeois tourist got up for a Hollywood film set'. Nevertheless, she managed a strained ideological leap into plain headscarves 'as a universal headgear' for women.

With that dam breached, she misread the compliant demeanour of workers as willing ideology, seemingly unaware they had been forced at the point of the bayonet from farm to urban factory, and agreed with 'no tipping' because it was 'an insult to workers'. Nonetheless, this visit by the Irish Friends of Soviet Russia was a brave step domestically, incurring the hostile interest of the British and Irish establishments, which might explain why she was disposed to accept at face value the orchestrated visits to factories and farms.

Harry Kernoff, on the other hand, was less taken in because he understood Russian and spoke with many of the artists he met, through which seeped the malign reality. As artists are usually critical of society, he absorbed the harsher realities behind the official version of the Soviet state. But as an 'artist delegate' from Ireland, which had lent money to the revolutionary government, he muted his comments, as he donated drawings and brought home an extensive collection of Russian art.

On his return after almost two months, impressions found their way into his work, as he drew urban poverty with a new, raw hardness. Several new works featured unemployed men in Dublin and the depression of those for whom 1916 – and all that flowed from it – had made life poor. His sketches of shipyards, docks and factories became further skewed towards the muscular values of industrial production, accentuated by his experience of Russia where factories had replaced churches as objects of collective veneration.

Returning to work in Ireland required adjustment to a 'smaller canvas'. Having missed the RHA of 1931 by being abroad, he was disappointed when the 1932 hanging committee rejected works inspired by the USSR experience. He did not flounce away in umbrage but settled for two pieces of compromise – one a portrait of the playwright Brinsley McNamara and the other, from conversations with Russian scientists on futuristic space travel, *The Fourth Dimension*. That seminal work did not impress critics and puz-

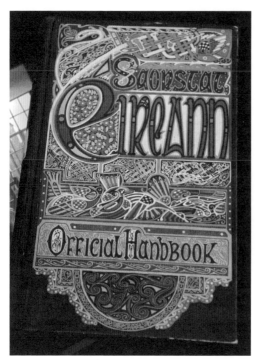

The Saorstat Éireann Official Handbook – Kernoff contributed to the cover with a mixture of Celtic and Jewish motifs

zled the viewers. The Russians may have destroyed their churches and replaced them with a mechanical idea of the heavens, but in Southern Ireland, the opposite was the case, as visual expressions of statehood made icons out of early Christian art (round towers and crosses) which were promoted as symbols of moral superiority.

Iconic use of the Ardagh Chalice, Cross of Cong and Book of Kells prominently featured in the *Saorstat Éireann Official Handbook* of 1932, designed to inflate the authority of independence. Later that year, as Eamon de Valera took over government, with his blithe recasting of Christian artefacts as official symbols of national life, hard-put artists played the official tune as they vied for commissions.

In the *Saorstat Éireann Official Handbook*, leading artists Sean O'Sullivan, Paul Henry, Sean Keating and Maurice MacGonigal delivered strong works of national imagery and received commercial exposure, as did Harry Kernoff to a lesser extent. Notwithstanding his graphics for left-wing publications, he was among the handful of artists who could be given state commissions, though not carrying the full DNA of being Irish and Catholic.

State commissions favoured Keating and MacGonigal as they romanticised the West of Ireland as an antidote to the official greyness of the East Coast, while Kernoff's versions were less sentimental. With an outsider's deftness, he steered clear of the ponderous question: how could a newly 'free' Ireland be defined visually, if artists painted only sixth century Christian ruins,?

It was a dilemma answered by painters periodically decamping across the Shannon to deliver romantic versions of aboriginal settlements. But as the inhabitants of these regions were the first to remark cynically as they took flight from poverty to Britain: 'You can't eat the scenery.'

If not eating it, state painters visually devoured it for a living, encouraged by their political masters deflecting economic failure into an idealised past. The values of bell, book and candle were inflated, though of little relevance to a population in need of food, housing and employment. Kernoff and colleague George Collie were among a handful to address these glaring gaps in official rhetoric. For all his romance with the West, much of Keating's work was cosmetic, using city friends as models for Aran islanders.

For Keating, such sleight of hand went in tandem with berating the 'poltroon politicians' for their duplicity, as he saw it, in attending art exhibitions to have their names mentioned in the press, while failing to fund art education. Keating, MacGonigal, Lamb and Henry were promoted as artists to fill vacancies in the national vista left by Orpen and Lavery, now almost wholly engaged abroad. Becoming more sour by the year, Keating put cowboy hats on some of his guerrilla fighters, satirising peasant drama and Hollywood films in a deft two-fingers. Though an accomplished figurative artist, Henry's bleak landscapes of Connemara were usually devoid of persons, but used by railways companies to lure tourists from grimy cities to depleted Ireland.

Keating delivered idealised clean milking parlours for creamery exports, leading one critic to wish that the painter's versions might improve the reality of Irish farming practices. In Britain

Making hay at Renvyle, Connemara

during the 1930s of mass hunger, the works of rural exaltation were a genuine artistic response to the failure of the Industrial Revolution to alleviate poverty – as in some British artists' depiction of bleak terraced slums, built for factory 'slaves'.

In their enthusiasm for the West of Ireland, imposing a breed of ancient Gael in a primal landscape, unspancilled by factory and urban terraces, many of the Irish painters followed Jack Yeats, who sat at the top of the pile of these Western enthusiasts. Stylistically ahead of the posse, adroitly adapting the 'isms' of modernist movements to his own poetic flair, he was the only one with authentic roots in the regions. As Yeats was found of saying, 'Sligo and the sky above it made me the painter I am'.

As a protege of both Keating and Yeats, Kernoff could not be immune from the West, though his forays into that landscape would bear his own style – rock-hard and geometric – the reaction of an urban painter confronted with sea and mountains. His innate impulses, sharpened by the Russian experience, now differed from Yeats, Keating, MacGonigal, Lamb and Henry. He was less in thrall to rural romance and, trusting his instincts, delivered unique works in what might be called 'Connemara out of Vitebsk'.

His stimuli were urban, his habitat the city of Dublin, his subjects the tasks of daily survival, as seen in pubs and coffee houses, music halls and at work in breweries and docks. His landscapes were rows of houses, his mountains the climbing inclines of tenements that ran up from the river Liffey towards Thomas Street and the Coombe, his valleys the small enclaves in the Liberties, traversed by natives of the inner city, pushing barrows of offal to dark caverns of hucksters' shops.

Kernoff tried 'the rural thing', out of collegiality with Yeats, Keating and MacGonigal, but it never quite took as he kept coming back to the places that formed him – the urbanscapes of London and Dublin. His artistic instincts would, in time, provide an archive of a vanished Dublin unrivalled in scale by any of his contemporaries.

10

Romances – and O'Casey

After the Russian visit, Harry Kernoff seemed incapable of staying at home for long periods, travelling frequently over the next few years, balancing – or failing to balance – demands of a life that was multi-layered. While Kate provided a staple of comforts – a warm home suffused with love and an elaborate dinner on the table – her interest in the romantic activities of an energetic son became irksome as a pattern evolved of sexual entanglements with married women.

He became circumspect about his private life, fielding questions with enigmatic answers, or cryptically saying he would be at so-and-so function and not to wait up for him. Invariably she did. Those who saw him home, sometimes unsteady after an evening of drink, heard, as they secured his key in the latch: 'Harry, is that you, Harry?' Kate in her chair in the front drawing room, with a view of the street, could not sleep until her favourite son, now a well-known artist in his thirties, was home. According to one account, the stress of having to hurry home became a joke among his lovers: 'Off with you, the Mammy will be waiting...'

Maybe that curfew helped Harry's prodigious output from his studio in Stamer Street and from outside locations, being well nourished in all aspects of his being, both outside and inside the home. By his mid-thirties, Harry was a familiar figure in Dublin, seen with a wooden valise which contained his sketchbooks, easily identified by his odd walk, described as 'a hop, skip and jump – like a little sparrow'. He became so much a part of Dublin life as a wanderer and observer that his colleague MacGonigal sometimes included him as an extra in crowd scenes.

Harry journeyed forth most days to see what might take his fancy, sometimes to the irritation of friends. MacGonigal recalled talks and walks meandering for miles, unable to fathom Kernoff's destination. The cliché of the wandering Jew aside, much of what is now lost from Dublin vistas, not available in photographic archives or newspapers libraries, may be re-pictured from his works, on a par with the claim of James Joyce that Victorian Dublin could be rebuilt from the topography of *Ulysses*.

From the available archive of work, by no means complete, it seems during the early 1930s that Kernoff was producing up-

St Stephen's Green, c. 1936

NO 9 (NEW SERIES) SEPTEMBER 1937.

A BROADSIDE

EDITORS: DOROTHY WELLESLEY AND W. B. YEATS.
PUBLISHED MONTHLY AT THE CUALA PRESS, ONE HUNDRED
AND THIRTY THREE LOWER BAGGOT STREET, DUBLIN.

THE LADY, THE SQUIRE, AND THE SERVING-MAID.

*A Broadside, September 1937, with a
Kernoff illustration*

wards of six different pieces in any one week, an output that amounts to a back catalogue of thousands. He worked, literally, across the boards – lino cuts and woodcuts; drawings in pen, ink and charcoal; oils on canvas, oils on board, oils on cardboard; watercolours on canvas, watercolours on cardboard and on paper; illustrations for magazines, books, theatre programmes; plus sets and costumes for plays and 'pageants'.

He worked for the Yeats sisters' periodical *A Broadside*, hand-printed pamphlets which published leading 'versifiers', which he, along with Jack Yeats, illustrated. He delivered graphics for anthologies of poetry and prose, for company publications and state reference books and civic guides. As well, he did sculptures in clay, plaster and bronze. Such output consolidated earlier promise and meant he had constant new material to show at exhibitions, his works each time being singled out for praise by critics and sought by patrons.

For all that, he was not, in the commercial sense, being 'collected' and regularly complained that he was earning just enough to live – which his friends understood as paying his way at home. He did earn enough to pay for gifts to Kate and his sister Lina, but for his extensive travels he depended on being regularly bought by stalwarts of Jewish community: doctors, lawyers and patrons in Dublin and his brother in London.

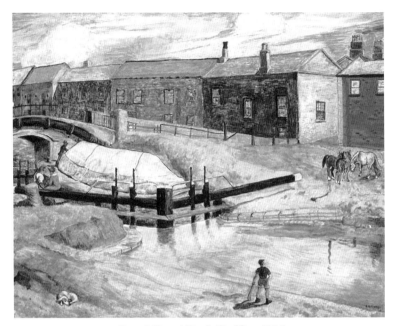

Grand Canal Dock, Dublin, 1935

Others of the time who bought at exhibitions or from his studio included former Republican activist Todd Andrews, then a state apparatchik as de Valera put his supporters into government jobs. Andrews occasionally ended an evening out with old comrades by visiting Harry in his studio and buying a work, ascending the attic in Stamer Street as energetically as he did state enterprises, paying from official budgets to decorate his office, as did Education Minister Tom Derrig.

In turn, the artist gifted works to those who promoted or helped his career, such as Conal O'Riordan, who opened a London show and received a watercolour of Dalkey Island. Toto Cogley received pencil and charcoal portraits, usually of herself, while those who helped him acquire commissions for a portrait of a matriarch or patriarch were thanked with sketches of religious relevance. For many families in Jewish society, having an artist in the community was a matter of pride, even if they would discourage marriage of their daughter to him.

In all of that annual output of a few hundred works across many media, he managed to keep active several romances in his thirties, primarily with Toto Cogley, but also diverted by 'flings' with actresses, dancers and singers. Apparently, such diversions served them both, relieving pressure from an affair whose longevity threatened domestic peace of both lives. Sometimes, too, travel out of the capital facilitated other liaisons.

During the early 1930s, Dublin formed an axis of his personal travels: London – Dublin – West of Ireland and back to Dublin via Kerry or Wicklow. Scenic works from those years read as a geographer's map of his travels. Several visits to London proved rewarding. Keeping in touch with the Kernoffs (Karnov) who lived there prompted a *Fairground at Hampstead*, the *Bend in the Road*, *Near Richmond* and *Euston Station*. This last painting sits symbolically atop the countries which made him, the rail terminus imbued with its brooding place in London life by whose sooty

Euston Station, London, c. 1937 – a brooding gateway of migration to the capital

Huband Bridge, Grand Canal, Dublin, 1936

pillars generations of immigrants trekked from Ireland, Scotland and Wales into the uncertainty of a new life in the capital. It's unlikely he could have cast it so tellingly, had he not been part of that diaspora.

With the experience of four solo exhibitions in Dublin, Kernoff was better equipped for another London exhibition, this time at Gieves Gallery in Bond Street in 1931. His invitees included art enthusiasts of the British and Irish establishments, as well as his extended family in London. Works were bought (some of no distinction) and the exhibition gathered glowing reviews in the London media.

A difference between himself and the playwright Sean O'Casey generated newspaper coverage days before the opening, as recorded in March, 1931 in the *Daily Herald*, a left-leaning newspaper, under the headline:

AUTHOR SPURNS HIS PORTRAIT

Two famous Irishmen, Sean O'Casey the playwright and Kernoff the Dublin artist, are throwing written brickbats at one another:

'I do not know Kernoff. He is a ballyhoo.' – O'Casey.

'The trouble with O'Casey is that he thinks he is a God.' – Kernoff.

The exchanges were over a portrait which Kernoff had completed from sketches and which the playwright did not like, comparing it unfavourably to the first version, bought by Lady Gregory for the Abbey Theatre. As O'Casey's public abandonment of Ireland and his attacks on censorship of his plays grew his fame, Kernoff produced versions to exploit the interest, showing an intensely focussed O'Casey 'lean and hungry' to the point of malnourishment – a version which on this occasion seemed to meld with the image of the 'playwright of the Irish Troubles'. The portrait in the Grieves Gallery was sure to arouse comment, given O'Casey's profile at the time. The *Herald* reported in dialogue that might have come from the playwright:

'I think the portrait is damn good,' wrote Mr Kernoff to Mr O'Casey.

'I think it is damn bad,' wrote Mr O'Casey in reply.

The paper had O'Casey denying he ever sat for the artist, 'for one second', with the artist replying that he had been welcomed on four occasions to the writer's home, had dinner with his family and had his permission to complete a portrait from drawings.

The exchanges rattled on for a few days, with Kernoff repeating:

O'Casey thinks he is a God and has a complex about his appearance – but I'm showing the Archangel Gabriel at the gal-

lery and I did not seek his permission and also the God of
War, and did not ask him ... O'Casey's portrait will be hung.

That seemed the end of the matter, garnishing useful public-
ity for the artist's exhibition. Later correspondence revealed that
O'Casey nurtured the hurt and referred to Kernoff as 'just the
kind of little tyke I thought you were...' Although they had known
each other in the 1920s since Kernoff's stage designs were lauded
for their realistic living quarters of slum-dwellers, by 1931 the
playwright still resented the Abbey's rejection in 1928 of *The Silver Tassie* and lumped together many from his native city, as if
somehow they could have forced the Abbey to recant.

Added to the playwright's vain dislike of his portrait was a
bitter disagreement over Russia, which O'Casey had many times
praised as a socialist model that other states should follow. Differences arose in reported comments of the other. O'Casey was at
a disadvantage, as he had not visited the reality, whereas Kernoff
had.

11

'Delia – Oh Delia!'

Travelling to the West of Ireland and London, free of the Mammy's monitoring, seemed to allow Harry Kernoff to develop a relationship with Delia Murphy, a ballad singer. Younger by a year, she was a handsome woman whose cheerful renderings enthralled both salon and music hall and whose personality was generous. They had in common parents whose married life had begun abroad and a capacity to make art out of the ordinary.

Delia was known for *Three Lovely Lassies from Bandon*, *Courtin' in the Kitchen* and other ditties of the Irish as a romantic people, 'poor but honest'. Her talent served many uses: being married to a diplomat corroborated the image promoted by the Free State, and her performances at concerts in world capitals created goodwill to be exploited for trade, tourism and bank loans.

That her husband's political function was committed to the international recognition of the Free State as separate from Britain provided both an elite audience for Delia and a leverage of domestic ease. Born in Claremorris, County Mayo of parents returned from America, Delia Murphy grew up in a mansion, Mount Jennings, which her father acquired with dollars made in the Klondike Gold Rush in the last years of the nineteenth century. Jack

Murphy was a robust character who thrived as shanty town populations doubled in months and fortunes were made and lost as celebrated in Robert Service ballads.

Murphy returned to buy a Big House in Mayo, thereby fulfilling the emigrant ambition in one of the large estates identified with British rule. The young Delia ran wild in Mount Jennings, made friends with travellers ('tinkers') on her father's land and was by all accounts a child of nature who learned songs later promoted as 'the music of the people'.

She learned ballads from travellers from a culture about to expire. Jack Murphy did not stint on his daughter's education. She went to convents and on to Galway University, where her looks and happy nature were not lost on a fellow student destined for the diplomatic service. When she married Tom Kiernan she was also marrying into the formal life of duties as her husband pursued a rising career through many capitals.

Consular missions were crucial to a new state not entitled to embassy status, being within the British Commonwealth of Nations but intent on further separation from British 'dominions beyond the seas...' In lobbying opinion-makers, Tom Kiernan and Delia became active, hosting receptions for tenor John McCormack and W.B. Yeats, recently become Nobel Laureate, and were benevolent patrons to Harry Kernoff's exhibitions in London. The mutual attraction between the wife of the diplomat and the artist went back to their time at the Gate Theatre in Dublin and was given energetic liaison in London's expanse.

By 1935 he was the age of the century with the tastes and curiosities of the time, though familial ties limited prospects of a married life of his own. After romances foundered on the realities of his Jewish background, he found sexual compliance with needful married women more agreeable than with single Catholic girls, whose tribal expectation of marriage were as strict as Dublin's Jewery. Both cultures held a disregard for artists as marriage material.

He had seen fellow artist Patrick Tuohy and his fiancé stressed by unforgiving families because of different religions. Similar attrition would be invoked were he to think of 'crossing the divide'. Even within the arts community, in theory free-thinking, tribal class divisions were strong, as there was mutual suspicion between the artists of Ascendancy pedigree and the Catholic class, which regarded the former as 'West Brits'.

Currachs, Connemara

Harry and Delia shared the outsiders' disdain of those labels, and were able to meet as her husband's immersion in demanding consular work gave her free time in London and Dublin. The 'Bohemian Set' provided camouflage in the moveable feasts which perambulated between a litany of Dublin pubs – the Palace Bar, Neary's, the Bailey and Davy Byrnes – hostelries where afternoon sessions could easily extend into the following morning. And unlike many Irishmen, Harry remained amorous in spite of a glass or two of absinthe being his favourite tipple.

The relationship was also facilitated by Delia's independent work rota, allowing her lover's journeys to venues in the regions. Harry seems to have spent an overnight in Westport, to meet a delayed Delia, and to fill the time delivered charming studies of the town's bridge, commissioned by a hotelier. Other points of rendezvous brought him to Galway, where he painted the Spanish Arch and Claddagh, home of an ancient fishing community, and to Renvyle in Connemara, which produced a stark rendering of *Launching the Currachs*, in homage to Paul Henry's version, by then a well-known travel poster. Kernoff's version is spikey and geometric in contrast to the fluid line of Henry.

How he squared his Delia-inspired travels with Toto Cogley is not fathomable, though correspondence suggests a rift around that time. It's not clear if he indicated to either married lover that he might 'someday' become a replacement husband. The times were against divorce, even for those of the artistic community, as a colleague in the theatre, the playwright Denis Johnston, found when his income as a barrister was severely curtailed by the official reaction to divorce. Generally, long-term adulterous relationships were tolerated providing homes were not broken up.

As we have seen in Kernoff's case, the Jewish community mitigated against marriage for him, a factor in the letter to the board of his old art school at the end of 1934, advocating it should lobby the government for a regular wage for artists in return for an agreed number of completed works.

He had in mind the Russian state wages for works of art for 'the glory of the proletariat'. Such Irish state subvention, he wrote, would be sufficient 'to allay (artists') fears of starvation, to allow them to marry, so they can work unhampered and produce their best works thereby'.

If stable income as a foundation for marriage was on his mind – who knows, maybe he seriously thought of either Delia or Toto

Phoenix Park, Dublin 1932

– the times were against him as an economic downturn contracted his father's business and the Mammy's likely strictures could be imagined.

Instead, he increased his already prodigious output to provide for Kate and Lina, as neither woman was in the modern sense working outside the home. As Isaac ailed and the brothers departed, Harry, it seems, was expected to fund the substantial home in Stamer Street, where the best of everything was kept. Food, especially, was generous, with Lina liking lobster and Kate displaying the best cuisine in a home she kept on a reduced income.

Whatever the pressures, his dedication did not diminish, to judge from the quality of the works produced during the mid-1930s – a veritable deluge of portraits, landscapes, illustrations and sculptures. The Medici Society in London bought *Birches, Phoenix Park*, for reproduction as a print, while the Cuala Press enterprise of the Yeats sisters periodically published his graphics. During 1935 he was elected an Associate of RHA in recognition of a decade of relationship with that body.

Though not intended as 'artistic displacement' of a frustrated love life, his eight RHA hangings that year were inspired by females and reflected a wider panorama of living than his contemporaries. The modernist *A Vortex* presaged European portents of war (Toto as model); the portrait of Madame Despard was a nod to his co-delegate to Russia; there were portraits of a matriarch of a Dublin merchant family, Kathleen Gunning, plus two marriageable daughters, Josephine Dunne and Patricia Skelton; and from his travels came a portrait of Peig Sayers of the Blasket Islands, which promoted the rural idyll most artists were expected to depict.

The latter was painted in Dunquinn, County Kerry where Kernoff stayed with the family of Sean Kavanagh, whom he knew from Davy Byrnes pub in Duke Street, Dublin. A scholar whose massive dictionary of Gaelic words preserved a dying language,

Kilbride, County Wicklow, 1933

Kavanagh was keen that Kernoff taste life on the coastal tip of Ireland.

On this Kerry safari, Kavanagh facilitated Harry to do portraits of Kruger Kavanagh and Padraig de Brun, using strong brushwork to emphasise their character as Mighty Men – to use a local phrase – who impacted upon the arts and national life of the 1930s.

Delia accompanied him on some of these journeys into the outposts – some would maintain the heart – of his adopted island, which were ancestral echoes of his parents' rural Belorussia.

12

Of Portraits, Piety and Cubism

arry Kernoff's election as a full member of the RHA towards the end of 1935 signalled an endorsement by that venerable institution, and also marked a midpoint of the standard working life, though it did not materially improve his earnings. While happy to add RHA after his signature, he had to work harder to keep earnings above subsistence level. The 1930s were fraught times in most of Europe, with economic collapse presaging political disaster. Southern Ireland, increasingly nervous that external hostilities might threaten its fragile independence, reached for theatrical displays to bolster nationhood.

The 1932 Eucharistic Congress was a high point for many, with massive religious gatherings in the Phoenix Park, the ten-year old Army in ceremonial salute to Papal emissaries and the capital's main artery turned into an elaborate altar. Gender-division proved effective crowd control as ceremonies were attended by a quarter of a million men one day and 200,000 women on another. With divorce banned and the printed media firmly under control, prolonged religious pomp defined the Free State as Catholic, with cabinet ministers bending the knee to corpulent cardinals.

Columns of newsprint listed hundreds of clergy, advertising pages promoted books of piety to saints held to be extra responsive to pleas from Ireland. Merchants profited, a few printing houses made vast sums and catering establishments were stretched to feed half a million pilgrims. Top brass of the Army and Gardaí accompanied the religious, and at evening muscular laymen patrolled for 'obscene literature' and 'immodest behaviour' – all an outpouring of piety that concealed the state's ongoing persecution of homosexuals, single mothers and the poor.

Southern Ireland during the 1930s evolved along the lines of Italy and Spain, with militant zeal that brooked little tolerance of other religions. While a few of its rulers publicly praised Mussolini and Franco, with whom they shared ambitions for militaristic power, they had neither the confidence nor the technical means to become fully Fascist.

An Aspect of Superrealism, or Floating Cubes

Where did this leave Harry's co-religionists? Marginalised to say the least – and wary of triumphalist Catholic power as hostile to their interests. Political connections with the new government helped soften prejudice, as a few Jewish families had participated in 1916 and were remembered by an incumbent Fianna Fáil government which still went by the name of the Republican Party. Harry, functioning on the fringes, negotiated minefields with his usual dexterity.

Abstract

Keating, now effectively a state artist, and MacGonigal sent minor commissions his way, including design for a postal stamp in 1932.

For artists, movements other than religious took priority. Experiments in style and 'ways of seeing' characterised the 1930s as Cubism, Surrealism and Abstract art challenged the academic tradition, whose defenders responded with hostility. Though evolving from distinct schools abroad, the differences blurred as they were interpreted in Ireland. Mainie Jellett, for instance, repeatedly urged her fellow artists to 'open your eyes to other shapes'.

Responding experimentally to the movements of fashion, Kernoff provided cubes, prisms and geometrical shapes which contained sly jokes. Discussing *Floating Cubes*, he challenged viewers to calculate the number of 'cubes' on view – a task that might test any reader today. Whatever number was calculated, he revealed another – joking that the 'banker always wins'.

Portrait of Flann O'Brien

Playing games with colours such as the Irish tricolour and communist red showed how easy it was to compose pieces of 'cubism', and betrayed his contempt for fashions which negated the academic tradition. For instance, he told friends to use naval signalling codes to decipher one of his 'cubist colours'. 'Up the Irish Workers' Republic' was the semaphore message of the collage.

Harry was, in the wider political sense, marginalised by Modernism, seeing it as appealing even less to customers' budgets. It's not surprising that he was occasionally miserable at the fall in earnings, or that he spent more time in the company of Baggot Street boulevardiers, a moveable group of fantasists who buoyed each other with wit and alcohol to keep despair at bay.

From those depressed times he has left us portraits true to the era: Eamon Martin, Spud Murphy, Tom Casement, 'an Irish Volunteer', the singer Gerald Croft, Army Commdt Fitzgerald. He did portraits of jarvey men and coster-mongers, of drinkers and of 'hard' men – all skilled to suggest the hidden history behind an apparently random study.

From the 'standing army of artists', colloquially known in Dublin as 'piss-artistes', he delivered vivid portraits of the 1930s, including the surgeon and wit Oliver St John Gogarty (model for Buck Mulligan in *Ulysses*), poets T.F. O'Higgins, Donagh McDonagh and Patrick Kavanagh, actor Barry Fitzgerald, writer

The Lavender Man was a favourite of Harry's, capturing a well-known Dublin character who according to legend sold 'fake lavender and real condoms'. He had a busman's bag and the packets of 'lavender' was a way of subverting the ban on condoms imposed by the new Free State during the 1920s at the behest of the Roman Catholic Church – a ban which lasted until the 1980s.

*The Tailor and Ansty – victims of risible
censorship in Ireland of the 1940s.*

Train in Ukraine – woodcut, 1930s.

Forty-foot bathing place, Sandycove, County Dublin which features in Ulysses *– note the
walking stick, hat, artist valise and towels which indicate the artist's presence – and absence.*

Mespil Road, by the Grand Canal, with a labour agitator at a corner meeting, 1930s.

Light, shade and shadow – view of stables from Kernoff's attic in Stamer Street, Dublin 8.

Self-portrait, 1927

Self-portrait, 1941

Bloomsbury Cafe 1930s, including G.B. Shaw, Virginia Woolf, Clive and Vanessa Bell, 'the bounder' Frank Harris and others of the Bloomsbury Set. Kernoff probably invoked artistic license as it's unlikely they were all together in this cafe in Holborn, London.

Carol Singers – used as a Christmas card

Trap the Tramp, Nova Scotia, 1957

Byzantine Madonna – Toto Cogley as model

Bathers, Naylor's Cove, Bray. A large oil on board containing more figures than will be likely counted at first sight. Held to be one of the artist's great works, it is in the European tradition of hard edge architecture as then pioneered by German 'New Realists' of the 1930s.

Donabate Beach, with light on the strand near side and rain across the bay far side.

The County Manager – woodcut

Detail from 'Let Us Work' – woodcut of unemployed protest, 1930s

A Funeral in Mayo – in the shadow of Croagh Patrick this watercolour manages to be sombre, sad and noble.

Couple watched over by proprietor of MacGillicuddy's Bar, Killarney, County Kerry – watercolour, 194

The Family under the Metro, artist concealed by nearside woman – Paris 1930s.

Liam O'Flaherty, novelist Benedict Kiely and playwright Lennox Robinson.

In a city of many cultures easily traversed in a day's walk, Harry met writers, lawyers, businessmen, poets and paupers and portrayed whatever took his fancy. Some he caught before fame froze them in the public image, such as the tousled-headed Brendan Behan, captured as a 'broth of a boy' before his drink-fuelled exploits lurched him to international notoriety.

Today these portraits form a rare record of the era, showing the movers and shakers in their prime,

Portrait of W.B. Yeats

ungarlanded by posterity. As in his landscapes, they hold a harder edge than the prevailing fashion. Compared to Osborne and Orpen, or to contemporaries Keating and MacGonigal, his portraits glint with realism rather than the Irish way of softening a personal portrait.

The critic S.B. Kennedy puts him in the school of German Realists of the 1930s, known as the *Neue Sachlichkeit* or New Objectivity, which set the pace of modernism during the inter-war years, displaying 'a cold descriptive linear style', and whose counterpart in Italy, *Pittura Metafisica*, 'was a superficial expression of a deeper trend towards the understanding of reality'.

It's hardly accidental that the art of those countries abandoned the curves of the Renaissance for the inflexible lineal order in public buildings, reflecting the Rise of Fascism. This presaging by art of militarism may have puzzled Kernoff – but it's salutary now to

From left, Martin Murphy, carpenter of the Gate Theatre, with Davy Byrne,
owner of the famous pub in Duke Street – the artist can be seen in the back

look at some of his portraits, showing the hardened features of
IRA gunmen, now bereft of promise, or the empty-pocketed despair of the unemployed – and compare, for instance, the harshly
lineal woodcut of the poet W.B. Yeats, whose military solution
to social problems was expressed as, 'Down, down, hammer them

down/Hammer the Fool and the Clown,' composed as a marching song of the Blueshirts.

In such a context, Kernoff's portraiture may be taken as adjunctive to his urbanscapes, infused with empathy for his subject, as in Liam O'Flaherty against the skewed cottages of Aran, or his Davy Byrnes set-pieces, with the proprietor as principal character and the artist himself as a casual extra.

He inserted himself into urbanscapes, often as a shadowy figure in wide-brimmed hat as in *Christchurch Hill.* Of that classic Davy Byrnes set-piece, it's no accident that Martin Murphy was the set builder in the Gate Theatre, or that another in that series has Davy Byrnes as seen directly from the Bailey on the other side of the street – the composition is influenced by the cinema director Alfred Hitchcock who regularly cast himself as an unimportant bit player, while being the creator of the entire scenario.

It was a joke which Kernoff repeated in major works. In crowded streets and beaches, look for the figure in a broad-brimmed hat or beret, sometimes as a shadow, sometimes in rear-view, sometimes led by a poodle and carrying the valise of sketch pad and pencils, the giveaway clue to his role as creator of the scenario. Yes, you have found him, the painterly author on the fringes...

13

Paintings of the Depression

War in Europe wrought crisis upon the Free State in relation to its former coloniser. While accepting that by 1939, Britain had to summon all its resources to resist the sweep of Nazism across Europe, premier de Valera felt that neutrality, though likely hazardous to hold, was the only course that could preserve internal peace while allowing its citizens to join British armed forces.

To have formally aligned itself with Britain in the war effort risked provoking the IRA to revive its campaign of internal sabotage, as that organisation was already embarked on a bombing campaign in England, in a foolhardy effort to force withdrawal from Ulster, where British garrisons were already being increased – and would be joined by Americans – to defend against German flotillas in the North Atlantic.

Treading a balance between British demands to make southern Irish ports accessible to shipping convoys and threats from Republican extremists, the Irish Free State declared an 'Emergency' while of 'being neutral on the side of Britain'. Ties of language, blood and acrimony proved more telling than neutrality.

Artists, as much as plumbers, farmers and shopkeepers, struggled to earn a living, as the state's economy closed down. Some artists joined British forces, some cowered at home under neutrality, while some, previously sceptical about Modernism, now embraced its 'subversive' tenets as prophetic to the end of civilisation. Thousands of Renaissance art works, which Modernism challenged, were plundered by Nazis.

For that coterie of Irish artists shielding on the most Western island off the beleaguered coast of Europe, illustrative work for a nervously neutral government provided income during the 'Emergency'. For Kernoff, whose racial background was obvious, the neutrality of his adopted country was reflected in his self-portrait with a tin hat and uniform of the local defence force modelled on Britain's Home Guard. Though a brother joined the Irish Navy, Harry never formally signed up as the hapless look he has given indicates what a poor military defender he would have made.

Being Jewish in a country unwilling to confront Nazism, an artist in a depleted economy, a left-winger in a right-wing Free State – it's salutary how much of 1940s Ireland found expression in his work. Long before this war, *Shalom* (Peace) had become his personal mantra, often doodled in decorative work on gifts.

As the State turned inward to its bogs and farmers increased production, Harry travelled West and South. He painted a Turf Girl in Connemara, quiet farms

Emergency, 1941 – 'Wot? Me a soldier?'

93

with sparse cattle, and horse jarveys in Killarney – all a rare rural record of the 1940s showing a country at peace, an absence of crowds and a stillness over the land.

Those works were praised by critic Thomas MacGreevy for *The Irish Times*, reviewing his exhibition at the Studio Club in 1942, where the artist's versatility was noted. Wondering if there was a 'Kernoff formula for excellence', the critic answered his own query:

> His talent is elastic in its application: scattered cottage in Connemara and rows of ribbon-built houses in Dublin...

Stating that Kernoff had a 'quicker eye for the pictorial possibilities of the things he sees than almost any other of our artists', MacGreevy noted the penchant for the 'eccentric and out-of-the-way types', especially in his drawings and woodcuts, and wondered if he might be more frequently employed as a 'mural decorator'. If this query was directed at ecclesiastics who gave commissions, it fell on deaf ears, for Kernoff's background put him outside the list of favoured painters for Church works – Keating and MacGonigal held the lion's share of commissions to deliver an idealised version. Nonetheless, he was among those invited to submit work for the pavilion of the Irish Free State at the 1939 New York World's Fair.

Plan for the Irish Pavilion at the New York World's Fair, 1939

Kernoff's return to Dublin was marked by an angrier tone, as shown in *Misery Hill* (1943) in which he records the despair of a man who props his arse against a wall, a common posture of the times, his entire demeanour one of defeat. Other men, no better off, are followed by Kernoff's cheerful poodle, a common whimsey in his work. Another man carries a sack of coal while a woman pushes a handcart of offal stew, another woman passes a poster Vote Labour.

The area known as Misery Hill was on a long stretch of road faced by men from slums hoping for a day's work unloading ships. Unusual for the time, its realism was of a poverty largely ignored by most of his contemporaries, with the exception of George Collie. Indeed, it may be seen as another iconic painting, given the official denial of such poverty. Those that lived on state salaries were consoled by the emigration of males, a safety-valve on civic unrest. These particular paintings by Kernoff did not prove popular.

In time, the district of Misery Hill would become so painful to urban planners as to be razed during the Celtic Tiger boom years of 2000, replaced by a New Dublin of hotels, walkways and desirable apartments with sea views – modelled on the Wall Street area of New York. But even that became fatally prescient as a model in the financial downturn of 2008, when the grandiose schemes were abandoned as the country coped with bankruptcy.

By then, unfinished office blocks and the stark skeletons of bank buildings loomed over Misery Hill as totems of the downturn. Two generations connected the mass depression of the 1930s to the recession of 2008 with inevitable emigration and a return to the social misery for which the district was originally known – though not on the same scale, as the EU bailed out the country, kept the unemployed on social welfare and sustained conditions which were immensely improved from the 1930s.

Speaking of misery, an act of censorship in the early 1940s caught Harry Kernoff's attention. Described by the writer Frank O'Connor as 'a remarkable old couple who lived in a tiny cottage on the mountain road up to the lake at Gougane Barra', the Tailor and Ansty relished their turn of phrase and had a gift for reducing both world history and national politics to local entertainment. Another writer, Eric Cross, recorded some of the merriment in conversations which they conducted for visitors and locals. When his accounts were published in a book, *The Tailor and Ansty*, the Irish Censorship Board judged it 'in general tendency obscene' and prohibited it from circulation. Three priests visited the isolated cottage and forced them to burn their only copy of the book – which led to their home being attacked by vandals and a virtual boycott by the community of the husband and wife. Kernoff's sympathy is expressed by his warm portrait of the harmless couple (see second colour plate section).

14

The White Stag Group
and Living Art

Back in 1939, as the Free State closed down under threat of war, some of its leading painters sought sanctuary along the West coast, retreating from a bomb-threatened capital into Celtic Twilight – an imagined vista at odds with the reality of most Europeans during war. But many of the farming and fishing men of the West into whose villages they fled had left to enlist in British Forces. In such depleted landscapes the artists missed the seismic upheaval that ravaged continents and would end with the Allied bombing of Japan, intended as ultimate deterrent against Fascism.

Insularity meant most Irish artists missed the movements which gained pace during the war. In painting, women artists showed more mettle with forays into Modernism by pioneers Mainie Jellett, Evie Hone and Nano Reid, whose support for another group of war refugees helped spawn a Modernist movement in Ireland. The White Stag group were made up of conscientious objectors to the war who sought refuge along the Western coast, some around Killary harbour in County Galway, though it is unlikely they knew its deep fjord was marked on naval maps of the combatants in the event of Ireland being invaded.

The refugees enjoyed a year of relative peace there, though they were objects of suspicion to the Garda Special Branch being British, German and French. When they moved to Dublin and produced amalgams of line drawings and engaged in lectures on psychotherapy, they generated frisson in the artistic community and alarmed academic artists with their take on 'subjective art' which they promoted as 'new ways of seeing'. Add lectures in damp Georgian basements under such headings as 'The Achievement of Expression' and 'What is Reality', and one can appreciate how bizarre they seemed in wartime.

Genuine in their intellectual pursuits, idealistic in the quests for meaning in a fracturing world, they promoted diktat of the mind over artistic matter. 'Meditate before applying the brush – then go with the flow' was one of their catch-phrases. Reaction to their exhibitions ranged from hostility to praise, as their theories influenced native artists, including Patrick Scott and Eddie Maguire. Living in the Baggot Street area, the Group meshed with other artists in studios of bright, airy rooms with large windows in decaying Georgian houses. The White Stag Group brought stimulus to a gloomy capital whose lights in every sense were dimmed.

Inevitably, in a city which cut pretension down to street level, they became known among the boulevardiers as the White Shag Group, a sly reference to its members' unconventional lifestyles, as some were homosexual, and others pursued multiple relationships. Many were also prone to drug taking, which they claimed produced artistic expression but left an aftermath of depression, and some would kill themselves after leaving Ireland when confronting the wasteland in Europe. What they did leave behind as an artistic movement is hard to quantify now, though in supporting the Living Art they diminished the magisterial control of the RHA, which had determined standards for over a century.

Responding to these eddies of fashion with badly scanned verse – and occasional experiment – Harry Kernoff did what he did best when upset, he got on with his daily output. By his early forties he had chalked up two decades of annual showing at the RHA and could command annual one-man exhibitions. In a city spending less on paintings than most capitals in Europe, he managed to earn a living by his willingness to take any commission – as crucial to his earnings as his modesty in undertaking every kind of work

Any output might include designs for theatrical shows, painted backdrops for suburban venues and basement cabaret for which Dublin was known – all in tandem with woodcut versions of his popular oils and watercolours He delivered original graphics for magazines and book publishers, did mini-versions of the more popular as greeting cards upon which for an extra five shillings he inscribed a buyer's name.

Publishers Cahill, whose man income came from school text books, found the quality of his woodcuts sufficient to produce a

Currachs, Connemara

handsome edition, bound in grey linen, with an essay by the country's most respected art critic Edward Sheehy, which astutely connected Kernoff's Russian heritage to explain skills distinctive from his contemporaries. Thirty-four woodcuts featured in the Cahill publication, including a rare self-portrait, which formed the frontispiece, the quality of which could only be achieved by woodblock, as noted by Sheehy:

> We see a definite affinity between (his) work and that of the modern French and Russian woodcut ... free and dramatic. While preserving a fine and modern composition, he harks back to the directness and naiveté of the early days of the craft before its degeneration in the hands of the 19th century illustrators.

This last was a reference to the mass production of engravings by 'hot metal' printing of the Industrial Revolution.

Claiming that the mechanical printing press had killed the medieval art as the sole means of reproducing drawings, Sheehy celebrated Kernoff's collection as being directly taken from original woodblocks and the care overseen by the printer. He went on to praise Kernoff's qualities of woodcut: 'with mastery of composition, the results are nearly always bold and dramatic'.

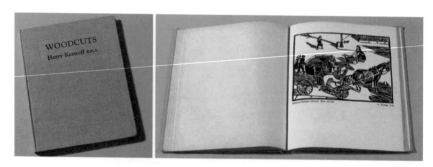

Three collections of woodcuts were published by
Cahills and Three Candles Press

On the debate in Europe about wood-cuts, Sheehy admired Kernoff's dexterity with the nature of the wood, which determined the finished work, citing the long facial lines of W.B. Yeats and the furrowed gloom of Casement, the artist literally going against the grain and sometimes with it – a citation that unwittingly took account of the creator's apprenticeship to cabinet-making.

Metal Bridge, Dublin, 1940

Sheehy endorsed his surmounting 'the limitations of a medium that does not lend itself to subtlety', praising *Peasant Woman*, *Man with a Pint* and *Public Meeting*. Looking at those now, over the rim of more than half a century, they absorb the antiquity of Albrecht Dürer on a lesser scale – not dragons of mythology but unique versions of life as lived in Dublin during the 1940s. No other artist of the time could do woodcuts like Kernoff.

Nor was Sheehy's praise confined to the artist's stamping ground:

> We think of him as stirred most easily to creation by the movement of people (to) pubs, grocers' shops, factories and steam-filled quays. Rowing the Currachs, Blasket Islander, get so exactly the flavour of the country-dweller...

Foreign critics had been impressed by Kernoff's take on coastal communities, noting his 'skewed' perspective as different from the 'sitting army' of Irish painters. With the praise of Sheehy for this collection, Kernoff showed he could as distinctively depict the hidden Irelands as artists ranked above him in public profile. But his heart and his head were in Dublin and its urbanscape continued to provide the bulk of this work.

As his difference was increasingly recognised during the 1940s, it's surprising he did not take to the Living Art movement, which would become the strongest alternative to the RHA. One might have assumed sympathy to its aims: 'To make available to a large public ... significant work of contemporary artists irrespective of school or manner.' One might have assumed his innate difference from the mainstream would see him in that company. Not the case...

Either he did not submit works for approval or resisted being marginalised by another 'rebel' movement, being essentially conservative in his own character. Maybe he felt sufficiently well done

Ringsend, Dublin, 1930s

by RHA, which had hung him generously. By 1943, the launch year of the Living Art, he had done reasonably well out of a decade of RHA exposure, save for the years of his Russian odyssey, 1930/31.

The launch exhibition of Living Art featured two works each by Mainie Jellett and Evie Hone, Jack B. Yeats hung three, while one by Louis le Brocquy had been rejected by RHA. Keating's tipping trucks at a power station reflected his genre of a country industriously renewing itself, in this case with electricity from natural resources, while (then) little-known Gerald Dillon's child-like scenes set the scene for his highly individual style.

Apart from the stature of the exhibitors, the patrons of the first Living Art exhibition included Dermod O'Brien, President of RHA, thereby blunting antipathy from that august body. As Jack B. Yeats' 'radical' works were backed by Victor Waddington's commercial support it seemed there might be coexistence between the two bodies.

Unusual also for the fractious times was the patronage of a government minister who happened to love paintings. In his role as Education Minister, Thomas Derrig gave pupils a free day to attend the Living Art. The longer-term results are probably incalculable as many who made careers as artists received inspiration in their school-free tour of the venue in 1943.

15

Nova Scotia

As the Free State became the Irish Republic during Easter 1949, little had changed in the welfare of is citizens, who emigrated in droves. As Europe became energised by post-war building, its most westerly state lay in a trough of despond, as seen by its artists and writers. Cutting a sprightly path through the prevailing mood, Kernoff kept up his output across the genres. By 1956, for instance, he had missed only two RHA annual exhibitions in over thirty years, and outside of that venue managed an annual solo show which sold increasingly well. By his mid-fifties he was a respected fixture on Dublin's artistic scene.

That milieu provided mere subsistence for visual artists. On top of the pile, so to speak, were le Brocquy, Keating and MacGonigal, while the Holy Trinity of leading prose writers O'Connor, O'Faolain and O'Flaherty lived by international magazines and teaching at American universities. For painters of Kernoff's middling rank and unusual style, few such opportunities presented for paid travel.

That changed with a chance encounter with a visitor from Nova Scotia, Albro Ettinger, in the Bailey pub in early spring of 1957. Ettinger's primary reason for being in Dublin was to tease out with premier Eamon de Valera constitutional issues of the

Men Fishing, West River Falls, Nova Scotia, 1957

British Commonwealth as Nova Scotia was an early colony to be-come self-governing in the nineteenth century. Ettinger was also an art enthusiast and, according to one version, the conviviality of the Bailey encouraged him to lobby de Valera the following day to sit for a portrait by his new-found Dublin friend.

Not only was a sitting agreed and a charcoal portrait of de Val-era purchased by Ettinger, but in its aftermath he invited Kernoff to an expenses-paid sojourn in Nova Scotia, which in painterly terms offered an expanse of sea-light upon its subjects. There was also a deeply personal matter in that Delia (Oh Delia!) had moved to Canada to support her husband's diplomatic posting in Ottawa and had signalled to Harry her loneliness for his company.

With those pressing incentives he assured Kate he would be gone only for the summer and duly arrived in the capital Hali-fax and the hospitality of the Ettinger household, which opened many doors to patronage and an exhibition of his watercolours, which in turn were generously reviewed. A portrait of Dublin

*Portrait of Gerard O'Brien, 1958 –
complete with scar*

book dealer Gerard O'Brien, replete with scar from a pub fight, took the fancy of a local newspaper which eventually photographed O'Brien to test the authenticity of the scar. A winsome portrait of Abbey actor Barry Fitzgerald, by then an established Hollywood character actor, gave Kernoff a profile which translated into fees as other 'Dub-alin' paintings caught the local imagination.

The patronage of Ettinger gave access to local subjects, including lumberjacks, fishermen and farmers, and one, Manuel Rivera, was related to the Mexican muralist Diego Rivera. While his personal meetings with Delia are shrouded in family discretion, the summer months produced a distinctive portfolio of over fifty paintings.

These ranged across his honed skills – watercolours in which he gave generous light refracted off waterways, as in *Fisherman at Shad Bay* and the strong character 'Trap Johnston', the country's legendary tramp, in *Hobo, Halifax*. People at work attracted him to *The Edge of the Circus*, a richly atmospheric view of performers in breaks between acrobatics, and *The Citadel, Halifax* with people going about their adventures of the ordinary.

What distinguishes his Nova Scotia output is light, permeating his watercolours with a playful toytown tone to public buildings and sometimes a pinkish hue as a cheerful change from the brown brick of 'dear dirty Dublin'. Vistas of public gardens in Halifax and silver birches in parks are similarly lightened. Even a

Parade and Citadel, Halifax, 1957

rare still life, *Gladioli*, is whimsically lighter than his usual palette. Presumably that cheerfulness lay in being away from home, the generosity of the host household and the time with Delia Murphy. By whatever feeling, he delivered a substantial portfolio over a few summer months whose full impact was shown at the Dublin gallery of Richie Hendricks during the following spring, about a year after meeting with Albro Ettinger.

Forty-four of the pictures were hung by Hendricks, the remainder having been gifted or sold in Nova Scotia. His Irish followers recognised the familiar span – urbanscapes of streets and parks, workers at ports, fishermen by rivers, citizens going by churches and town halls – his little creatures going about their tasks in another mosaic of his eternal village, this time in the sealight of Halifax.

This perspective was challenged by *The Irish Times* critic who lambasted him for painting 'in the broad light of noon when the light is strong and the shadows are harsh ... to paint pictures at this time of day … needs flawless craftmanship…' The critic signed as C.H.G. was not enamoured of the portraiture but found the cityscapes and vistas attractive, notably *The Citadel, Halifax,* 'the vague, old fashioned aspect making both cars and clothes look like relics of a by-gone age'. To which the artist might have added: 'Precisely!'

Harry could afford to be sanguine as his summer labour sold at the Hendriks Gallery and, in the wider perspective of his life, detaching himself from Dublin had been worthwhile in capturing fresh light and in spending time with Delia.

16

Of Doggerel, Death and Mr Spock

Conscious of attaining his sixties even as contemporaries succumbed to alcohol and ills of mind and flesh, Harry Kernoff became more introspective and morose. Some of his demeanour may be accounted to private losses of romantic relationships, mainly with married women who, when push came to shove, stayed with their spouses or terminated the relationship as becoming tawdry, difficult or threatening to their married status.

Consigned to past passion were the cabaret artiste Toto Cogley (*Desiree* and other works) and the intense, reciprocated passion for the singer Delia Murphy which similarly imprinted herself on his heart and canvas. About half a dozen others were known as fleeting sexual partners, among them two actresses from the Abbey Theatre. A more recent object of consensual passion was a painter whose husband took objection to the relationship and brought about its end. According to one credible account, Harry was given a 'duffing' near his home.

For all that, he was still attractive to women but less inclined to embark on long-term relationships. He seems to have become resigned to the single life as he turned sixty, with decades of full-time artistic endeavour behind him and years of output across various media – oils and watercolour, woodcuts and graphics, charcoals and line-drawings. He had become a familiar, respected figure in the Dublin art world, frequently admired in his annual solo exhibitions and RHA outings.

Still, his state troubled him and sometimes sought release in complaints, though his account books of the time show steady annual sales in excess of the average industrial wage, sales which he meticulously recorded alongside expenses of electricity and heating bills. He joined arts lobbies asking government to provide a basic stipend for artists, 'which would thereby allow them to marry and raise a family'. It was a heartfelt cry in his case: he remained a maverick Jewish artist who was not a 'good bet' as husband in his own community while the prospering Catholics retained similar resistance across the religious divide.

Harry's sister, Lina, unmarried, had assumed a primary role as homemaker with his mother, both proud of his achievements and solicitous for his welfare. His indulgence in absinthe was a prob-

Portrait of Lina, Harry's sister

lem, as neighbours regularly saw him unsteadily negotiate the steps of the family home. On a periodic London visit, an apparently routine letter from Lina mentions weather and wishes him well but warns, 'be careful (you know what I mean!') Kate fretted during his absences and on his return was keen to hear all his news: he was forthcoming about their relations but discreet about his romantic rendezvous, London being a traditional gateway for illicit passion among the Irish middle classes. When in Dublin he was expected home by mealtimes. His brothers had made their own way in the world. Bernard ('Barney') after a long stint studying medicine had gone to London where he worked in a trade-union sponsored hospital for manual workers – again a reflection of that humanitarian streak in the family. His eventual family became regular visitors to Stamer Street, finding a hospitable home away from home.

Harry's brother Bernard with his son Peter

Another brother, Kay '(Hymie') negotiated his own way though the sensitivities of Dublin life. Family photographs show him in the naval reserve during the Second World War, a meaningful service to their family's adoptive state when it was uncertain that southern Ireland might be invaded. He became involved with a young Dublin woman who was not Jewish. Their relationship, strongly romantic, lasted their lifetimes.

The way in which his siblings had settled left Harry more isolated in his sixties. Kate still operated a warm, well-run family home in which he and his unmarried sister were destined to becoming senior citizens with 'neither chick nor child'. Such status was common enough in the Ireland of the 1960s, though the country's nearest neighbour was in thrall to upheavals in mores and manners that would become known as 'The Swinging Sixties'.

Those seminal sixties in Britain also saw revolutions in technology and visual media, with spin-offs in theatre and TV helping to demolish the Old Order. Many artists and writers publicly

Harry's formidable mother Kate, with his sister Lina

criticised Britain's Suez debacle ('last gasp of an Empire'), mocked the established church and adjusted the focus of women's fashions to the crotch. Art schools speedily absorbed technical advances in acrylics and photography to produce Pop Art. While accepting the merits of Academe and Renaissance, art fashions moved rapidly through the 'Moderns' and on to burgeoning Abstract Art, loosely defined as 'a language of form and colour without reference to visual reality'.

Harry Kernoff, academic by training, innovative and modernist by instinct, became obsessively opposed to Abstract Art, penning diatribes in the public prints and doggerel for private circulation – a hostile stance in some degree reflecting where life had placed him in his sixties.

A Dublin exhibition during the summer of 1963 provoked him to an outpouring of extended doggerel, badly-scanned, opening with a broadside:

> Billious, amorphous, gangrenous muck
> Negative, crapulous, on canvas stuck...

From his descriptive repertoire, came other gems of abuse:

> A pile of incomprehensible junk,
> Coprolitic, scatological punk...

And so on, reminiscent of Joyce's 'Gas from a Burner', sans the wit and rhyming scheme of his fellow Dubliner (as Harry now so regarded himself).

> A bloke in Paris because he was broke
> Painted a joke with the tail of a moke
> Awarded a medal of gold
> – then speedily sold...

He had words for the 'creators' of such art:

> With draughtmanship nil and colour-sense vague
> This lack of design would give you the ague...

And for the purchasers, whom he contrasted with the ordinary buyer:

> The Man in the Street whom they've set out to rob
> Goes into the show with his humble few bob
> Meets with the upstart society snob
> And the noveau-reech, black-market mob...

Enough to drive one to drink, he concludes, though like many patrons of the Dublin pubs he did not need the stimulus of Abstract Art to enjoy his pub life. A cartoon around this time shows him among the literary clientele of the Palace Bar, near the office of *The Irish Times*, a paper which reviewed him generously and gave space to a fervid debate on Abstract Art.

Dublin evening papers also indulged the debate which ran for weeks, a reflection of it readers' need for periodic distraction to subjects of no economic relevance at a time of poverty. Art trends had a strong following not confined to the bourgeoisie, and evening papers gave a platform to populist debate. 'Standards in Art' was the heading under which Kernoff argued against a current fashion:

> While there had always been abstract art, most was meaning-
> less... Art had to represent something, which Abstract Art
> failed to do, other than being decorative or mood enhancing.

'Dublin Culture' by caricaturist Alan Reeves shows writers and artists in the Palace Bar – Harry Kernoff is in the middle of the table in the front

Delivering a crash course in Art History to readers of newspapers, he noted:

> In recent centuries, Art subordinated the aesthetic to the anecdotal – a reference to scenic paintings of privileged family narrative – but the craze for abstract was not a substitute: 'Given no title, an abstract would have no clue to what it is...

As on many previous outings, he championed the 'aesthetic integrity' of the artist and the judgement of history.

Harry quoted children – which featured in his streetscapes – as being better judges of art than adults – citing the fable of the Emperor's New Clothes. His public campaign was no tilting at windmills or an eccentric voice in the wilderness of fashion, as he had embraced experimentation before most contemporaries in a futuristic vision of how Space and Time defined human species. A daring work based on the success of the Russian-launched Sputnik satellite of the late 1950s, it was an artistic response to

114

scientific advances. As we now know, the Sputnik programme pioneered by USSR galvanised America into the Space Race and while billions were spent to bankrupt the Soviets, the wider worlds of medicine, science, visual technology and communications were the beneficiaries.

In terms of populist impact, one experiment in portraiture dating back to the 1930s was to have a 'spatial influence' well beyond any Irish visual image of the times. As 'Oirish' as a double

Dublin Children – often featured in Harry's urbanscapes

portrait of two vintage pint-drinkers in a pub (Fat Man and Thin Man) the work spawned global imagery when the Thin Man was adapted for lead character in a television series. The Fat Man was an amalgam of two people – Davy Byrne, proprietor of the pub, and the Lord Mayor of Dublin Alfie Byrne – while the Thin Man was concocted from Martin Murphy, the set-maker at the Gate Theatre and 'The Toucher Doyle', a cadger who allegedly touched a visiting English king for the loan of a fiver. Somewhere in there also was an uncle on his father's side.

Titled *A Bird Never Flew on One Wing*, in homage to the buying your round custom – 'You'll have another, you will you will – sure a bird never flew on one wing' – the painting was also a celebration of pub names embedded in the background. Proving a more authentic image of Ireland than harps and round towers, it was instantly recognisable to denizens as their own place. As it became widely admired as a large oil on board, the artist produced copies as wood-cuts and, in response to more requests, he painted two other oil versions.

The original, hanging in a pub near Leeson Street in the early sixties, caught the eye of a visiting designer for a futuristic series of a television drama. The symmetry of hairline, eyebrows, pointed ears and high cheekbones of the Thin Man took his fancy and returning to the studios in Culver City, he doodled a lead character for the first series of *Star Trek*, then in development and influenced by the space programmes of the US and USSR.

Within months the features of the Thin Man, heightened in a space-travelling humanoid called Mr Spock, caught viewers' imaginations. By the late-sixties the series *Star Trek* had become a global hit spawning a franchise industry of comics, products and books to a ready market in any country that imported American TV series. It would become the most successful drama in the history of an industry a mere twenty-five years old and long after Kernoff's time it continued to generate billions of dollars.

A Bird Never Flew on One Wing

Mr Spock's appeal lay in the visual extensions of familiar facial features, a likeness absent in previous renditions of aliens, as they tended towards the monstrous. Initial parental resistance in millions of living rooms changed to enthusiasm as Mr Spock's capacity for logical thinking became as potent an educative tool as school books. As to the unwitting spawner of a global character, the monetary value to Kernoff appears to have been nil. Though the connection was noted by aficionados of the artist, owners of the *Star Trek* franchise were wary of formally acknowledging their debt, probably for reasons of legal copyright.

According to Ted Morrison, onetime designer at the studios, the connection of Spock to Dublin was known:

> A story from the back lots of Culver City was that Mr Spock was inspired by a painting that hung in a Dublin bar – having seen the painting, the resemblance is astonishing...

Amusingly enough, both models were known to the artist and drawn from life. Yet even as *Star Trek* was taking off, so to speak, the originator's life was being dented with monetary concerns as his account books showed him chasing buyers for payment or return of works.

Irony may be heaped on irony here – the walls of his attic studio in Stamer Street were lined with portraits of writers then in their prime who would make an impact. Some would make international reputations, some were in the course of such, yet so were little regarded at home that Kernoff, who had pursued them for portraits mainly without fee, was left with them lining his studio. And in spite of the revolution of 1916 generating celebration from politicians who owed their privileges to that time, there was little commercial take-up of his woodcut portraits of James Connolly and Roger Casement.

To such an extent that Kernoff gifted 'a new print of Casement in the dock' to James White, Director the National Gallery, noting in a letter that it was done from an original photograph. 'How it was done I do not know, it was passed to me by some clandestine IRA during the 1930s...' He gifted other rare material around the same time in early 1966, wrote further doggerel with a deepening introspection and pondered both his own future and the collection of portraits.

They were reminders of a life well lived in good fellowship and artistic endeavour in 'rare oul' times', to speculate from a photograph of him in situ with his notables, most of whom he had known in the pubs of Dublin and, in the case of James Joyce, in the cafes of Paris. The photography shows a distinct proprietorial pride in his creations but now he wanted rid of them...

His misery was heightened by the death in the previous months of one of his early and great loves, Madame Toto Cogley, creator of a cabaret which began life in an art gallery and went on to became a ground-breaking venue during the 1920s, and with whom he had embraced a personal and professional adventure. Obituaries noted her role in the Revolution, her subsequent theatrical innovations, her founding of the Gate Theatre with Edwards and MacLiammoir, her disillusion with how Ireland evolved and her departure to London where she tried to repeat her theatrical style.

Potted histories of the Studio recalled the rarity of the fare and the unusual decor. Round the walls were pinned cut-out heads, nearly all of them done by Harry Kernoff, of artistes, poets, playwrights... One of the chief diversions was to discover who was the latest recipient of the honour (of being pinned to the wall). Toto's death at 82 indicated she was seventeen years older than Kernoff, which he may not have known, given the world of illusionary theatre into which she had initiated him. Cards found among her private effects indicated affectionate feelings towards him that lasted her lifetime.

This recall of the Studio Cabaret – and its decor – weighed upon his mood towards his collection which featured some from that era and later versions of O'Casey, Johnston, MacNamara, O'Flaherty, Behan and Kinsella. He had about thirty-six portraits of the 'shakers and movers' in the arts and political world from the time the state was being formed and after it mutated into a Republic. As exhibitions saw no takers, he began a correspondence with James White

Portrait of Sean O'Casey

in December 1966, offering the entire collection to the National Gallery:

> ... 36 of them that I have done from James Joyce to Brendan Behan they are all framed and similar to the one I lent the Gallery of Piaras Biaslai ... it's a pity to break them up as a set and I offer them to the National Gallery of Ir. for £1,000 ... I am yours sincerely, Harry Kernoff, RHA
>
> ps mostly drawn from life but I knew them all – HK

That letter valued the portraits at £28 each and White replied a week later, offering £25 each for twenty of the portraits, half what the artist hoped to get, though for near half the number. He accepted, tentatively asking if the Joyce and Behan might be included.

The negotiations rested over Christmas but in February of 1967 he received a cryptic letter from White:

The question of the portraits in your possession has been raised with the Board and for the moment they do not wish to pursue the matter. However we can discuss it again when we meet. Yours sincerely, James White

The rejection was yet another of the 'slings and arrows' that periodically affect most lives, in Harry's case coming on the heels of Toto's demise and when the cycles of art fashions were moving away from his style. Art students of that time – admiring his work as part of their studies – recall him as being gruff and complaining in the coffee-houses near the school. Sensing how he must seem to a younger generation, he penned more doggerel:

> Please do no forget I am sixty-eight
> These years do no invalidate
> Personality that makes me man...
> Biologically I can – and I plan
> Freud: Happiness is release of tension

The verse contains coded personal feelings, citing Freud that he was still sexually active. According to one source who knew him well at that time:

> Whatever his cranky image, he held an extraordinary attrac-
> tion for some younger women. I had arranged to meet him
> one evening, he was late and I went to the office of a solicitor
> where he told me he would be earlier ... the office had closed
> but the door was open and I came upon Harry and a secretary
> hastily doing up their clothes ... they had been on the leather
> couch in reception.

Intimations of mortality hastened. Dependent upon glasses he now faced severely diminishing eyesight with the knowledge it was crucial to his art and life. A more telling blow came in November 1969 when Kate died. More than anyone she had been his adroit, guiding light and in ways unique to mothers had provided

Two aspects of Winetavern Street in the shadow of Christchurch Cathedral – in the bottom one we see a backview of the artist jauntily descending the hill, in the top version he is climbing back up on a stick. Kernoff did many versions in oil and watercolour as it proved a good seller to visitors.

Jewish man and an Irish countrywoman

*Harry Kernoff, proprietor Davy Byrne of the famous pub and Martin Murphy,
carpenter at the Gate Theatre – one of several done in this location.*

Absinthe Drinker – the potent liquor, a favourite of the artist, was held to induce changes of sensory and visual perception, but at 70% proof was eventually banned in many countries.

Actor Cyril Cusack and theatre diarist Joseph Holloway in watercolour, chalk and crayon

Trinity College lecturer A.J. Leventhal who effected introduction to James Joyce in Paris

Sean Kavanagh, Republican and Gaelic scholar

A Connemara Turf Girl – her features influenced by Kernoff's Western muse. Delia Murphy.

'Tinker' encampment, Dolphin's Barn, Dublin

Resting horse cabbie, corner Baggot Street/St Stephens Green

Sean O'Casey, author of plays which gained worldwide recognition. Intense, unkempt and hungry as seen by Kernoff – a portrayal that angered the playwright.

Oliver St. John Gogarty – wit, physician and raconteur, aka Buck Mulligan in Ulysses.

'Be Jaysus I'll hew yer beauty be the sweat of me brow' – pastel cartoon of the sculptor Des MacNamara attempting to set in stone the aura of Madame Toto Cogley.

Woodcut of Mayo colleen as influenced by his relations with singer Delia Murphy from Westport.

THE · GREATEST · THING · IN · THE · WORLD · IS · THE · DIVINE · IMAGINATION
· THE · CROCK · OF · GOLD ·

Toto Cogley as the model for the Fairy Queen in designs for the play 'The Crock of Gold'.

Misery Hill, Dublin in the 1930s invokes men returning from docks where they failed to get work. Mainly now demolished and replaced by the current skeletal, bankrupt buildings of the current recession.

him with support beyond what was visible. She was buried in the Jewish Cemetery in Dolphins Barn in the grave that had been created for her husband Isaac, and which now marked the passing of two parents whose arrival in Dublin in 1914 began a family name that would celebrate the Irish capital beyond their own existence.

Harry Kernoff's headstone in the Jewish Cemetery, Dolphins Barn

17

Valediction

Aspects improved for Kernoff in his seventies. A tax concession on earnings – for which he had long campaigned – was applied to him through the good offices of an official who admired both his art and his politics.

When Sean Collins, polo-playing proprietor of the Godolphin Gallery, mounted 'Harry Kernoff – a Selection of Dublin Paintings' during the spring of 1974, he shrewdly chose John Ryan, the onetime proprietor of the Bailey pub, to write what would become a panegyric for the artist. As painter, writer and sailor as well as pub proprietor – a Renaissance Man of which Dublin had a notable number – Ryan delivered a critique that placed the artist in the centre of the capital's life.

> From Stamer Street has issued a continuous flow of paintings of the great, the curious, the famous and the notorious, playing their various roles and wearing their particular plumage … whether it was the 'Toucher' Doyle who actually borrowed a fiver from King of England at Fairyhouse Races or Endymyon with his cricket bats (*Ulysses*) or the Lavender Man who sold fake lavender and real French Letters (condoms) … or the Pope O'Mahoney or Oliver Gogarty (*Ulysses* again)

He was 'our Boswell in Paint' – for the fresh way he looked at the physical city with streets, shops and houses, lanes and alleys, bridges, crescents, churches, pubs, theatres. Whether a mansion or a crumbling tenement he made it a glowing affirmation of affection ... W.S. Lowry is the only other painter who matches the radical humanism he shows in his portrayal of the urban environment in which so many of us spend our lives.

Mick Price, Jarvey, Killarney

For all his rootedness in Dublin, the artist's forays into the regions North and South were not ignored, as Ryan opined:

> He depicted a Killarney Jarvey with the same warmth and honesty as he did an Apprentice Boy from Derry. He has commemorated us memorably.

It was an endorsement echoed by leading art critic Brian Fallon of *The Irish Times* who said that in him, 'Dublin had found its small-scale Utrillo'.

Apprentice Boys of Derry

If comparisons are held to be odious, it is probably that in Harry's case he was not bothered at being placed somewhere between the classical Utrillo and the modernist Lowry. He was – and in his art is – entirely his own man. As presaged in one of

Winetavern Street, Dublin

his verses: 'Time will separate the good from the bad/the dross, the abstract, the mad.' As reminded by his friend MacGonigal, they had seen the tides of fashion go in and out a few times – a prophetic judgement as it turned out after Kernoff's death when the main body of his output, amounting to thousands of works, bucked the market and became collectors' items at soaring prices while some of his seminal pieces such as *Naylor's Cove*, *Winetavern Street*, various scenes of *St Stephen's Green* and his views of *Davy Byrnes* pub fetched prices way above those of most of his contemporaries.

Neither Ryan nor MacGonigal were to know it would be the artist's last exhibition in his lifetime. Mortality overcame other events planned to celebrate him, including an appearance on *The Late Late Show*, the nation's favourite television outing. The slowing down he had presaged came to its natural end on Christmas Day, 1974 when he succumbed to a heart attack having been taken to the Meath Hospital near his home. The funeral at Dolphin's

Barn Jewish Cemetery was in the part of Dublin he loved and where he had painted circuses and traveller encampments. The Chief Rabbi was represented among an attendance that included the President of Ireland, Cearbhall O'Dalaigh, and the President of the RHA (former fellow student Maurice MacGonigal). Chief mourner was his sister Lina. Others came to form an unfestive congregation in a festive time, providing a collection of 'subjects' from the city he had unwittingly adopted, and whose fabled diversity he had faithfully recorded.

Index

Sources

As this is not an academic work there are no footnotes to distract from the narrative which is organised chronologically as a handy way of relating the artist's life. The information linking those segments comes mainly from family, friends and colleagues of the artist, augmented by coverage of exhibitions from the main media of the times, as well as catalogues, book illustrations and publications.

Specialists interested in sources are directed to the main reference libraries mentioned in the Preface and to the many publications which give insight into the period. The following are worth reading for relevance:

- *A School of Art in Dublin* by John Turpin, Gill and Macmillan, Dublin 1995

- *The Irish Counter-Rvolution, 1921-36* by John M. Regan, Gill and Macmillan, Dublin 2001

- *The Boys* by Christopher Fitzsimons, Gill and Macmillan, Dubln 1994.

7/2186238.